KETO COOKBOOK FOR

TWO

2 Books in 1: Activate Ketosis and Lose Body Fat in 21 Days by Consuming Low-Carb Food Easily Prepared by Following 83 Mouthwatering Recipes for Two

KETO COOKBOOK FOR WOMEN

KETO COOKBOOK FOR MEN

KETO COOKBOOK FOR WOMEN

Table of Contents

Introduction ------------------------------------- 13

Keto Meals Recipes For Women---------------- 16

45+ Recipes------------------------------------- 16

1. Bacon-Wrapped Jalapeno Poppers ------------16

2. Low-Carbohydrate Slow Cooker Vegetable Soup--18

3. Keto Caesar Salad ----------------------------21

4. Cajun Chicken Salad With Guacamole --------23

5. Keto Cheeseburger Salad----------------------25

6. Instant Pot Cauliflower Soup - Keto, Low Carb------ ---27

7. Low-Carbohydrate Stuffed Pepper Soup -----29

8. Recipe For Chicken Kale Soup----------------31

9. Keto Gumbo ----------------------------------33

10. Asparagus With Dutch Sauce (Brown Butter) 35

11. Keto Creamy Cauliflower Vegetable Soup ----38

12. Keto Tzatziki---------------------------------40

13. Keto Spinach Dip-----------------------------42

14. Keto Mayonnaise Recipe ---------------------44

15. Low-Carb Broccoli And Bacon Croquettes ----46

16. Delicious Vegetable Medley ------------------49

17. Keto Fruits And Veggies For Women----------52

18. Low Carb Keto Yogurt ------------------------55

19. Keto Cheesy Vegetable Bake------------------58

20. Keto Green Veggie Skillet --------------------60

21. Easy Keto Brownies ----------------------------62

22. Chocolate Keto Protein Shake ----------------64

23. Fried Salmon With Thyme Ghee And Cucumber Nodles --66

24. Easy Baked Tandoori Salmon With Cauliflower Rice--68

25. Keto Double Chocolate Muffins----------------71

26. Cookie Dough Keto Fat Bombs ----------------73

27. Keto Cheese Bread For Women ----------------75

28. Crab And Zucchini Casserole ------------------78

29. Keto Avocado Pops-----------------------------80

30. Bacon Pineapple Shrimp Skewers-------------82

31. Keto Stir-Fried Chicken -----------------------84

32. Grilled Salmon With Broccoli ------------------86

33. Grilled Flank Steak With Lemon Herb Sauce -88

34. Baked Salmon With Creamy Dill Sauce - Keto And Low Carb --------------------------------------91

35. Keto Cauliflower Bread -----------------------93

36. Chicken Meatballs And Cauliflower Rice With Coconut Herb Sauce---------------------------------96

37. Keto Yogurt Bark Recipe----------------------99

38. Low-Carb, Baked Kale, And Broccoli Salad - 101

39. Low-Carb Asparagus Salad With Walnuts -- 103

40. Low Carbohydrate Vegan Bowl-------------- 104

41. Keto Breakfast Parfait Recipe - Low-Carb Yogurt, Muesli, And Berries --------------------- 106

42. Keto Breakfast Parfait ---------------------- *108*

43. Low Carb Turkey And Pepper --------------- *110*

44. Keto Butter Chicken ------------------------ *113*

45. Keto Fried Bacon Omelet ------------------- *116*

46. Keto Chicken Wings With Creamy Broccoli - *118*

47. Keto Chicken Thighs With Mozzarella Cheese--- ----- -- *120*

48. Steaks With Mushroom Sauce -------------- *123*

49. Carb Keto Cheese Sauce Recipe ----------- *126*

50. Zucchini Pizza Crust ----------------------- *128*

Conclusion -------------------------------------**131**

INTRODUCTION

A ketogenic diet is a low-fat, low-carb diet intended to help fat digestion. At the point when the body runs out of glucose stores, it changes to utilizing fat and unsaturated fats, which produce intensifies called ketones. Ketones cross the blood-cerebrum boundary and enter the mind, where they are utilized as an elective fuel source.

Basically, it is an eating routine that makes the body discharge ketones into the circulation system. Most cells like to utilize glucose, which comes from sugars, as the body's fundamental wellspring of energy.

Since it needs carbs, a ketogenic diet is wealthy in proteins and fats. It ordinarily incorporates a lot of meats, eggs, prepared meats, wieners, cheeses, fish, nuts, spread, oils, seeds, and sinewy vegetables.

Cyclical ketogenic diets are more advanced methods and primarily used by bodybuilders or athletes. Carbs are the fundamental wellspring of energy for our body.

Without enough carbs for energy, the body separates fat into ketones. The ketones at that point become the essential wellspring of fuel for the body. Ketones give energy to the heart, kidneys and different muscles. The body additionally utilizes ketones as an elective fuel hotspot for the mind. On a Keto diet, carbs from all sources are seriously limited. Organic products are rich in carbs; however you can have certain organic products (typically berries) in little bits.

Vegetables (likewise rich in carbs) are confined to verdant greens (like kale, Swiss chard, spinach), cauliflower, broccoli, Brussels sprouts, asparagus, ringer peppers, onions, garlic, mushrooms, cucumber, celery, and summer squashes. A cup of chopped broccoli has around six carbs. With the objective of keeping carbs less than 50 grams each day, Keto weight watchers regularly burn-through no breads, grains or cereals. Furthermore, even foods grown from the ground are restricted in light of the fact that they, as well, contain carbs. Ketogenic meals carry huge importance for women who want to have less carbs in their diet.

Keto meals recipes for women 45+ recipes

1.   Bacon-Wrapped Jalapeno Poppers

Preparation Time: 25 mins |Cooking Time: 25 mins |Total Time: 50 mins | Portion: 12 | Calories: 198kcal

INGREDIENTS:

- 12 jalapeno peppers about 3-4 inches long
- 1 8-ounce block of cream cheese softened
- 1 cup of cheddar cheese
- 1/2 teaspoon onion powder
- 1/2 teaspoon of salt
- 1/2 teaspoon of pepper
- 12 slices of bacon, not sliced thick baking spray

DIRECTIONS:

1. Preheat the oven to 400 degrees. Line a baking sheet with foil and cover it with cooking spray.
2. Cut the jalapenos in half lengthwise and scoop out the seeds and ribs with a spoon.
3. In a medium bowl, combine the cream cheese, cheddar cheese, onion powder, salt, and pepper.
4. Fill each jalapeno half with the cheese mixture.
5. Cut the bacon slices in half crosswise and wrap each pepper in a slice of bacon. Use a toothpick to secure the bacon.
6. Divide the peppers over the baking tray and bake for 20-25 minutes until the bacon is crispy and brown. Serve immediately

2. Low-carbohydrate slow cooker vegetable soup

INGREDIENTS:

- Cut four slices of bacon into 1/2 inch pieces
- 2 pounds stew meat cut into 1 "cubes, pat dry
- 2-tablespoons of red wine vinegar
- 32 grams of low-sodium beef stock
- 1-medium yellow onion chopped
- Cut 1/4 cup green beans into 1-inch pieces
- 1-small celeriac (about 6 grams) cut into cubes
- 1/4 cup carrots cut into cubes
- 2-tablespoons of tomato paste
- 1-28-ounce can diced tomatoes
- Crushed 2-cloves of garlic
- 1/2 teaspoon of dried rosemary

- 1/2 teaspoon of dried thyme
- 1/2 teaspoon black pepper, freshly ground
- 1-teaspoon of sea salt

DIRECTIONS:

1. Heat a large skillet over medium heat. Add bacon—Cook the bacon, occasionally stirring, until crispy. Remove the bacon from the pan with a slotted spoon on a paper towel-lined plate. Cover the bacon and put it in the fridge for later.

2. Discard everything except about one tablespoon of bacon fat. Return the pan to the burner over medium heat. Add cubes of beef in batches, making sure they do not touch. Season with salt and pepper. Brown each side of the beef cubes. Do not cook meat. When the outside is brown, transfer the beef to the slow cooker with a slotted spoon. Repeat for the rest of the meat.

3. Once all the meat is browned and in the slow cooker, places the skillet over medium heat. Add vinegar to the pan. Stir and scrape brown pieces until the vinegar has thickened. Pour in about 1/4 cup of the stock and continue to scrape any browned bits—transfer liquid to the slow cooker.

4. Add the rest of the stock, onion, green beans, celeriac, carrots, tomato paste, diced tomatoes, garlic rosemary, thyme, salt (only when using low-salt stock), and pepper to the slow cooker. Stir gently.

5. Cover the slow cooker and cook on low for 6 to 8 hours. Taste and adjust seasoning before serving. Garnish with reserved bacon cubes before serving.

3.   Keto Caesar Salad

15 + 20 min | Serve 2

INGREDIENTS:

- Dressing
- Salad
- Chicken breasts, with bone and skin
- Bacon
- Romaine lettuce, minced meat

DIRECTIONS:

1. Set separately in the refrigerator.
2. On top of. Bake the chicken in the oven for about 20 minutes or until cooked through
3. By. You can also cook the chicken on the stove if you prefer.
4. Place the lettuce as a base on two plates. Top with cut
5. Chicken and the crispy, crumbled bacon.
6. Cheese.

4. Cajun chicken salad with guacamole

Time 20 + 15 minutes | Serve 2

INGREDIENTS:

- Cajun spice mix
- Chicken
- Sugar snaps
- (2 ¾ cups) arugula

DIRECTIONS:

1. Combine well. Cut the
2. Chicken into long strips. Brush with the spice mixture with the chicken and
3. marinate for at least 5 minutes (see tip)
4. Add the peas and cook until al dente. Drain well.

5. Cut the tomatoes into thin wedges. To do
6. This over a sieve and keep the juices for the vinaigrette pepper.
7. Put the pulp in a bowl and add the lime
8. Juice. Season with salt and pepper and mash until done.

5. Keto Cheeseburger Salad

Time 15 + 15 minutes | Serve 4

INGREDIENTS:

- Seasoned ground beef
- Dressing
- Pickles, finely chopped
- Salad
- (3 cups) lettuce, cut into smaller lettuce leaves
- pickle

DIRECTIONS:

1. Seasoned ground beef
2. Make use of one
3. spatula, mix and crumble the meat with the herbs, fry until brown
4. And cook for about 15 minutes.
5. Dressing
6. Salad tomatoes, garnish with beef, cheese, red onion, and pickles. Finish by drizzling the dressing on top.

6. Instant Pot Cauliflower Soup - Keto, Low Carb

Prep time: 5 minutes cooking time: 10 minutes

INGREDIENTS:

- Three cloves of garlic, peeled
- 6 cups of raw cauliflower florets
- One teaspoon of kosher salt
- 1/4 teaspoon ground black pepper
- 1/4 teaspoon ground mustard powder
- 1 1/2 cups grated cheese (horseradish cheddar)
- 4 ounces of mascarpone cheese
- One clove of garlic thinly sliced and fried in oil (optional garnish)

DIRECTIONS:

1. To make in the Instant Pot:
2. Combine the raw garlic, cauliflower, water, salt, pepper, and mustard powder in the Instant Pot.

3. Set to Manual / High / 10 minutes.
4. When you are done, bleed with the quick release.
5. Remove the lid after all steam has been removed. Stir in the mascarpone and grated cheese. Mix with a hand blender until smooth. (Or transfer to a traditional blender and blend until smooth.) Taste and adjust seasoning as desired.

7. Low-carbohydrate stuffed pepper soup

INGREDIENTS:

- 1 pound ground beef
- 1/4 cup sliced onions
- Two cloves of garlic, chopped
- Salt and pepper
- 3 cups of beef stock
- 1-green pepper, chopped
- 1-medium tomato, chopped
- 1-tablespoon of Worcestershire sauce
- 1/4 teaspoon of red pepper flakes
- 8 ounces of cauliflower in rice (about 2 cups)

DIRECTIONS:

1. Place the Instant Pot or another pressure cooker on the baking function. Once hot, add the ground beef and cook until mostly brown, dividing while cooking. Add the onions and garlic, season with salt and pepper, and cook for an additional 4 to 5 minutes, or until the onions are translucent. Stir in the stock, bell pepper, tomato, Worcestershire sauce, and red pepper flakes. Close the pressure cooker and put it on the soup function for 10 minutes. After the cooking time has elapsed, release the pressure manually and open the lid. Add the cauliflower rice, close, and set on the soup function for 3 minutes. Release the pressure manually after the cooking time has elapsed. Add salt and pepper to taste.

8.   Recipe For Chicken Kale Soup

INGREDIENTS:

- One tablespoon of olive oil
- 2 pounds boneless and skinless chicken breast or thigh meat
- 14 ounces of chicken stock
- 32 grams of chicken stock
- 5 ounces of baby cabbage leaves
- Salt to taste

DIRECTIONS:

1. Heat 1 tablespoon of olive oil in a large skillet over medium heat.

2. Season the chicken with salt and pepper and add to the heated skillet.

3. Reduce the temperature to medium, cover the pan and cook the chicken for about 15 minutes or until the internal temperature reaches 165F.

4. Chop the chicken and put it in a crockpot.

5. Process the chicken stock, chopped onion, and olive oil in the blender (I used a NutriBullet) until well combined. Pour into crockpot.

6. Stir the remaining into the crockpot cover.

7. Cook over low heat for about 6 hours, stirring once or twice while cooking.

9.   Keto Gumbo

INGREDIENTS:

- 3 lbs. boneless and skinless chicken thighs (I used those from my Butcher Box)
- 1 pound frozen shrimp, gutted, without tails
- 1 pound sausage, cut into rounds
- 1-bell pepper, cut into cubes
- 1-onion, diced
- 2-celery stalks, cut into cubes
- 4 t of garlic in olive oil
- 6 grams of tomato paste
- 15 ounces of diced tomatoes

DIRECTIONS:

1. Cook on high for 3-4 hours or on low for 7-8 hours.
2. Add the shrimp 20 minutes before serving.
3. Stay warm and enjoy!

10. Asparagus With Dutch Sauce (Brown Butter)

Preparation Time: 10 mins |Cooking Time: 5 mins |Total Time: 15 mins | Servings: 4 | Calories: 248kcal

INGREDIENTS:

- 1 pound asparagus, trimmed
- 1 tablespoon of water
- salt and pepper to taste
- hollandaise sauce
- 2 large egg yolks
- 1/2 teaspoon Dijon mustard
- 1 tablespoon of water
- 1-2 teaspoons freshly squeezed lemon juice (or white vinegar)
- 1-2 pinches of cayenne pepper

- 1-2 pinches of white pepper

DIRECTIONS:

Preparation:

1. If the asparagus is medium to large in thickness, cut an inch off the bottom and lightly peel the stems with a vegetable peeler. I start about 1/3 from the top and continue to the bottom of each spear. If the asparagus is thin, hold a spear down and bend it until it clicks. Cut the remaining spears to the same length. Separate the eggs and save the egg whites for another use.

2. Asparagus:

3. Place the asparagus in a microwave safe bowl and add 1 tablespoon of water. Cover with plastic wrap and cook on high power for 1 1/2 - 2 1/2 minutes, depending on your microwave. Drain the water and keep it covered. Alternating: blanch the asparagus in boiling water until crisp, drain and keep warm.

Blender Hollandaise

1. Add the egg yolks, 1 tablespoon of water, 1 teaspoon of lemon juice and the mustard to a blender. Put the lid on and remove the middle piece. Place the butter in a medium to large skillet and melt the butter over medium heat. Reduce heat to medium-high and gently swirl the pan every few moments. When the solids at the bottom of the pan are just starting to brown, turn off the heat. Set the blender on low and start pouring the hot butter into the blender, leaving the brown solids in the pan.

2. After the butter is incorporated, add the cayenne and white pepper and mix. Taste. Adjust seasoning with more acid, salt, or pepper. Pour over the asparagus and serve immediately. For 4 persons.

11. Keto Creamy Cauliflower Vegetable So up

Cooking Time: 20 mins |Total Time: 25 mins |

Servings: 32 bites | Calories: 337kcal

INGREDIENTS:

- 1 pound of cauliflower
- 1 cup of heavy cream
- 2 teaspoons of Salt
- 1 teaspoon pepper white, ground
- 1/2 teaspoon ground nutmeg
- 2 oz. butter salted

DIRECTIONS:

1. Cut the cauliflower into even sized pieces and put them in a pan

2. Add the whipped cream to the pan and fill the pan with water until only the tips of the cauliflower are above the water.

3. Bring the cauliflower to a boil and simmer for 10 minutes, until very tender and break apart easily with a spoon.

4. Add salt, pepper, nutmeg and butter.

5. Mix the soup with a hand blender, being careful not to splash yourself with the hot liquid. We recommend mixing in short bursts until the mixture is smooth.

6. Spoon the soup into 4 bowls to serve and enjoy.

7. Comments

12. Keto Tzatziki

INGREDIENTS:

- ½ (51/3 oz.) Cucumber
- 1 tsp. salt
- 1 tbsp. olive oil
- 1 tbsp. fresh mint, finely chopped
- 2-cloves of garlic
- 1 cup of Greek yogurt
- 1-pinch of ground black pepper

DIRECTIONS:

1. Rinse and finely chop the cucumber. You can also grate it with the coarse side of a grater. Do not peel the cucumber; the skin adds color and texture to the sauce.

2. Put a cucumber in a sieve and sprinkle with salt. Mix well and let the liquid drain for 5-10 minutes. Wrap cucumber in a tea towel and squeeze out the excess moisture

3. Crush or chop the garlic and put it in a bowl. Add cucumber, oil, and fresh mint (optional).

4. Stir in the yogurt and add black pepper and salt to taste.

5. Let the sauce sit in the refrigerator for at least 10 minutes to allow the flavors to develop. It can be kept in the refrigerator for about three days.

13. Keto spinach dip

INGREDIENTS:

- 2 tbsp. light olive oil
- 2 ounces. frozen spinach
- 2 tbsp. dried parsley
- 1 tbsp. dried dill
- 1 tsp. onion powder
- ½ teaspoon of salt
- ¼ tsp. ground black pepper
- 1 cup of mayonnaise
- ¼ cup of sour cream
- 2 tsp. lemon juice

DIRECTIONS:

1. Defrost the frozen spinach and remove excess moisture.

2. Let stand for 10 minutes for the flavors to develop.

14. Keto Mayonnaise Recipe

INGREDIENTS:

- One egg
- One teaspoon of Dijon mustard
- 2 tsp. white wine vinegar or lemon juice
- ¼ teaspoon of salt
- 1 cup of light olive or avocado oil

DIRECTIONS:

1. Break the egg into a tall and narrow mixing bowl, a large glass measuring cup or cup, and add the Dijon mustard, vinegar, and salt.

2. Place the immersion blender on the bottom of the container before turning it on. Start mixing with one hand and use the other hand to slowly pour the oil into the bowl in a thin, even stream as you continue to mix. Note that the bottom layer should turn white and creamy before you lift the blender to the next layer. The mayonnaise is ready when it is thick and fluffy.

15. Low-carb broccoli and bacon croquettes

Preparation Time: 20 mins |Chilling Time: 20 mins |Total Time: 1 hour| Servings: 14 Croquettes | Calories: 126kcal

INGREDIENTS:

- 1 pound of broccoli
- 2 oz. butter
- 3 slices of bacon
- 1/2 cup of grated parmesan cheese
- 1 egg
- 2 oz. pork rinds crushed into crumbs
- 1 teaspoon of salt
- 2 teaspoons of pepper
- 1 tbsp. Linseed ground
- 1 tbsp. almond flour

DIRECTIONS:

1. Boil or steam broccoli for 5 minutes or until tender, drain well.

2. Mix the warm broccoli with the butter into a puree. Place in a bowl and stir in the grated Parmesan cheese, pepper and salt.

3. Cut the bacon into small pieces and cook over low to medium heat for 6 to 8 minutes. The bacon fat will melt while the bacon is browning, add the bacon and fat to the broccoli and mix well.

4. Chill the broccoli and bacon mixture for at least 30 minutes.

5. Set your fryer to 350F / 180C and let it heat up.

6. After the mix has cooled, add the egg and ground pork rinds and mix well.

7. Roll the mixture into 14 small barrel molds.

8. On a plate, mix the almond flour and linseed flour, roll each croquette through this dry mixture, making sure each side is covered, then press the mixture onto the surface of the croquette.

9. Fry your croquettes in batches, so that you do not overfill the fryer. They will take about 3-5 minutes, remove when crispy and golden brown. To enjoy!

16. Delicious Vegetable Medley

INGREDIENTS:

- 6 tablespoons of olive oil
- 240 g baby Bella mushrooms
- 115 g broccoli
- 100 g sugar snaps
- 90 g paprika
- 90 g spinach
- 2 tablespoons of pumpkin seeds
- 2 teaspoons of chopped garlic
- 1 teaspoon of salt
- 1 teaspoon of pepper
- ½ teaspoon of red pepper flakes

DIRECTIONS:

1. Start cooking all of your vegetables. Cut the 115 g broccoli into bite-sized florets. Cut the 90 g bell pepper into strips and then finely chop the strips. If you're not using pre-sliced mushrooms, make sure to slice your 240g mushrooms in this too.

2. Add 6 tablespoons. Olive oil in a wok and bring to hot heat.

3. When the oil is hot, add garlic and let it cook for 1 minute.

4. Once the garlic starts to brown, add the mushrooms and stir to combine.

5. When the mushrooms have absorbed most of the oil, add the broccoli and mix well.

6. Add 100 g Sugar Snap Peas to the mixture and stir well.

7. Add your peppers to the bowl and stir well. You want the peppers to still be a little crunchy by the time you're done.

8. Add all your herbs: 1 tsp. Salt, 1 tsp. Pepper and 1/2 tsp. Red Pepper Flakes. Taste here and add more spices if desired.

9. Add 2 tablespoons. Pumpkins seeds and stir them into the vegetables.

10. When the vegetables are cooked, place 90 g spinach on top of the vegetables and let the steam reduce them.

11. Once the spinach has shrunk, mix everything together and serve!

12. This makes a total of 4 servings of vegetables, with each serving containing 235.5 calories, 21.2 g fats, 6.37 g net carbs and 4.26 g protein.

17. Keto Fruits and Veggies for women

Preparation Time: 10 mins |Cooking Time: 25 mins |Total Time: 35 mins

INGREDIENTS:

- 1 Cauliflower
- 1 bell pepper
- 1 cup mushroom slices, fresh
- 1 cup asparagus, chopped
- 1 tbsp. Olive oil

DIRECTIONS:

1. Preheat the oven to 400 ° F (205 ° C). Cover a baking tray with a silicone mat (or foil or baking paper).
2. Cut your cauliflower and bell pepper into equal sized pieces.
3. Slice your mushrooms and chop your asparagus.
4. Drizzle all your vegetables with olive oil.
5. Spread cauliflower, bell pepper, and mushrooms on baking tray. Don't crowd them and leave room for asparagus.
6. Bake for 10 minutes.
7. Stir / turn the vegetables and add asparagus to the pan.
8. Bake for 15 minutes, stir / turn again (after about 7 minutes).
9. Comments
10. The roasting times of vegetables are not 100% reliable. The larger the pieces, the longer it takes to cook.

11. If you want crispier roasted vegetables, shorten the roasting time by a few minutes. If you want softer roasted vegetables, increase the roasting time by up to 10 minutes (except asparagus, which should increase by up to 5 minutes).

18. Low Carb Keto Yogurt

INGREDIENTS:

- Keto Yogurt:
- 1/4 cup of almonds
- 2 cups of water
- 2 cups of heavy cream
- 1/2 tablespoon of gelatin powder
- 1/4 teaspoon liquid sunflower lecithin (optional, for texture and to reduce secretion)
- 2 Probiotic capsules (active cultures)
- Toppings:
- Eaton hemp hearts
- Sliced almonds
- Coconut chips
- Berries (raspberries, blueberries, strawberries)
- Sugar-free jam

DIRECTIONS:

1. Click on the times below to start a kitchen timer while you cook.

2. Sterilize 2 16 oz. jars in the dishwasher or with hot soapy water. Dry and set aside.

3. Use the almonds and water to make almond milk according to these (You don't need the vanilla and salt in that recipe unless you want to add them.) Don't use store-bought almond milk - the preservatives will keep your Keto yogurt from fermenting properly.

4. Place the homemade almond milk and cream in a medium saucepan over medium heat. Heat gently, occasionally stirring, for 5-7 minutes, until bubbles form around the edges. (Time can vary considerably depending on the material of your pan - mine was a cast iron pan like this one.) Do not simmer or boil.

5. Sprinkle (do not dump) the gelatin over the pan and beat until dissolved.

6. Remove from heat. Sprinkle with the sunflower lecithin and beat until dissolved.

7. Pour the cream mixture into the sterilized jars. Let the jars sit at room temperature for about 20 minutes until the mixture is below 43 ° C (110 ° F) but still above 100 ° F (37 degrees C). This is critical - a higher temperature will kill the probiotic cultures.

8. Open or cut a probiotic capsule over each jar and stir in the powder. Cover with lids.

19. Keto Cheesy Vegetable Bake

Preparation Time: 5 mins |Cooking Time: 50 mins |Total Time: 55 mins | Course: savory portions: 8

INGREDIENTS:

- 1 kg cauliflower broccoli, or any combination of vegetables of your choice (cauliflower, broccoli, zucchini, bell pepper, pumpkin, eggplant, mushrooms, [spinach, kale, asparagus - cook for 10 minutes only])
- 200 cheddar or prepared pizza cheese from 'Making it Simple' If using only mozzarella, add 1/2 teaspoon extra salt
- 4 tsp. Dijon mustard
- 500 sour cream
- 1/4 teaspoon of salt

DIRECTIONS:

1. Coarsely chop the vegetables and put them in the large Varoma steamer bowl
2. Put 500 g of water in the mixing bowl
3. Place varoma and steam 30 minutes / varoma temp / speed 3
4. Carefully remove the lid and make sure all vegetables are cooked, otherwise you have 5 minutes / VAROMA temp / speed 3 cooking
5. Remove the lid and set the varoma aside on a tea towel or on the sink to allow the steam and condensation to evaporate
6. Pour water from the mixer
7. Without washing the mixer, chop cheddar for 5 seconds / speed 5 / mc or use pizza cheese mix from 'Making it Simple'
8. Add Dijon mustard and sour cream, mix 5 seconds / speed 3 / mc
9. Pour the cooked vegetables into a large oven dish, pour over the cheese sauce and roughly stir through the vegetables
10. Bake uncovered at 180 ° C for 20-25 minutes or until golden brown

20. Keto Green Veggie Skillet

Preparation Time: 5 mins |Cooking Time: 10 mins |Ready In: 15 mins

INGREDIENTS:

- Zucchini
- 12 ounces
- (340 g)
- Olive oil
- 1 tablespoon
- (14 g or 0.49 oz.)
- salt
- ¼ tsp.
- (2 g or 0.07 oz.)
- Black pepper, ground
- ¼ tsp.

- Garlic powder
- ¼ tsp.
- Onions powder
- ¼ tsp.
- Thyme, dried
- 1 tsp.
- Butter, unsalted
- 1 tablespoon
- (14 g or 0.49 oz.)
- Spinach
- 3 ounces
- (85 g)

DIRECTIONS:

1. Cut your zucchini into quarters. Toss the pieces in a bowl with the olive oil and all the spices. Pour the contents into a saucepan over medium heat and cook, stirring occasionally, until the zucchini is soft and lightly browned.

2. Lower the heat on your stove and melt the butter in the pan. When all of the zucchini is covered, add the chopped spinach to the zucchini. Stir slowly while the spinach softens and mix in the pan. Cook the spinach to your liking - as wilted or fresh as you like!

21. Easy Keto Brownies

CAL / SERV: 260YIELD: 16 SERVINGS PREP TIME: 0 HOURS 15 MIN

TOTAL TIME: 1 HOUR 25 MIN

INGREDIENTS:

- 4 large eggs
- 2 ripe avocados
- 1/2 c. (1 stick) melted butter
- 6 tbsp. unsweetened peanut butter
- 2 teaspoons. baking powder
- 2/3 c. Keto-friendly granulated sugar (such as Swerve)
- 2/3 c. unsweetened cocoa powder
- 2 teaspoons. pure vanilla extract
- 1/2 tsp. kosher salt
- Flaky sea salt (optional)

DIRECTIONS

1. Preheat the oven to 350 ° and line a 20 x 20 cm square pan with baking paper. In a blender or food processor, combine all *INGREDIENTS:* except flaky sea salt and blend until smooth.

2. Transfer the batter to the prepared baking pan and smooth the top with a spatula. Sprinkle with flakes of sea salt, if using.

3. Bake for 25 to 30 minutes until the brownies feel soft but not wet at all.

4. Let cool for 25 to 30 minutes before slicing and serving.

22. Chocolate Keto Protein Shake

REVENUE: 1PREP TIME: 0 HOURS 5 MINTOTAL TIME: 0 HOURS 5 MIN

INGREDIENTS:

- 3/4 c. almond milk
- 1/2 c. ice-
- 2 tablespoons. almond butter
- 2 tablespoons. unsweetened cocoa powder
- 2 up to 3 tbsp. Keto-friendly sugar substitute to taste (such as Swerve)
- 1 tbsp. chia seeds, plus more for serving
- 2 tablespoons. hemp seeds, plus more to serve
- 1/2 tbsp. pure vanilla extract
- Squeeze kosher salt

DIRECTIONS

1. Combine all in the blender and blend until smooth. Pour into a glass and garnish with more chia seeds and hemp seeds.

23. Fried Salmon With Thyme Ghee And Cucumber Nodles

Start to finish: 20 minutes

INGREDIENTS:

- 2 5-ounce wild salmon fillets, with skin
- 1 fennel bulb, roughly chopped
- 1 large cucumber
- 1/2 cup of pitted green olives
- 3 tablespoons butter
- Fresh thyme leaves
- 2 tablespoons of extra virgin olive oil

DIRECTIONS:

1. Preheat the oven to 350 F.

2. Place fennel in a parchment-lined baking tray made of parchment paper. Place the salmon on the fennel and the ghee on the salmon. Sprinkle with fresh thyme leaves.

3. Bake the salmon in the oven for 15 minutes.

4. While the salmon is in the oven, turn the cucumber into noodles and drain excess water by squeezing gently.

5. Add the noodles to a bowl and dress with extra virgin olive oil.

6. Remove the salmon from the oven.

7. Transfer the noodles to a plate and top with the salmon. Add the green olives and sprinkle with salt to taste.

24. Easy Baked Tandoori Salmon With Cauliflower Rice

Start to finish: 50 minutes (20 minutes active)

INGREDIENTS:

- Two 4-ounce wild-caught salmon fillets
- 6 ounces of pure, sugar-free coconut milk yogurt
- 1 tablespoon of raw apple cider vinegar
- 1 tablespoon of avocado oil
- 1 teaspoon ground ginger, or 1-inch piece of mixed fresh ginger
- 1 teaspoon of ground turmeric
- 1 teaspoon of green cardamom seeds
- 1 teaspoon of Ceylon cinnamon
- 1 teaspoon of cloves
- 1 teaspoon of cumin seeds

- 1 medium cauliflower, cut into strips
- 1 tablespoon of coconut oil
- 1 spring onion, sliced
- 1 small carrot, sliced or spiral
- 1/4 cucumber, sliced
- 1 lime, cut into wedges

DIRECTIONS:

1. Prepare the tandoori salmon. Mix coconut yogurt with all the spices in a mixing bowl. Add the salmon to the bowl and cover. Marinate for 30 minutes (either on the counter if you plan to cook immediately, or in the fridge if you cook later).
2. Preheat the oven to 350 degrees. Line a baking tray with foil.
3. Remove the salmon from the marinade and place skin side down on the baking tray.
4. Bake in the oven for 5 minutes. Bring up your oven rack and roast the salmon for 2-3 minutes until a light brown crust is formed.
5. While the salmon is cooking, prepare the cauliflower rice. Heat a wide pan over medium heat and add the coconut oil, stirring to cover the pan.

6. Add cauliflower to the pan. Sauté for 3 minutes or until soft, then remove from heat.

7. Divide cauliflower rice between two plates and cover with salmon. Garnish with the rest of the vegetables and a squeeze of lime juice.

8. Makes: Serves 2

25. Keto double chocolate muffins

CAL / SERV: 280YIELD: 1 BOXES

PREPARATION TIME: 0 HOURS 10 MIN TOTAL

TIME: 0 HOURS 25 MIN

INGREDIENTS:

- 2 c. almond flour
- 3/4 c. unsweetened cocoa powder
- 1/4 c. swerve sweetener
- 1 1/2 tsp. baking powder
- 1 tsp. kosher salt
- 1 c. (2 sticks) butter, melted
- 3 large eggs
- 1 tsp. pure vanilla extract
- 1 c. sugar-free dark chocolate chips, like Lily's

DIRECTIONS

1. Preheat the oven to 350 ° and line a muffin tin with lining. In a large bowl, combine almond flour, cocoa powder, Swerve, baking powder and salt. Add melted butter, eggs and vanilla and stir until combined.

2. Fold in chocolate chips.

3. Divide batter among muffin liners and bake until toothpick inserted in center comes out clean, 12 minutes.

26. Cookie Dough Keto Fat Bombs

CAL / SERV: 70YIELD: 30PREP TIME:

0 HOURS 5 MIN TOTAL TIME: 1 HOUR 5 MIN

INGREDIENTS:

- 1/2 c. (1 stick) butter, softened
- 1/3 c. Keto-friendly confectioner's sugar (such as Swerve)
- 1/2 tsp. pure vanilla extract
- 1/2 tsp. kosher salt
- 2 c. almond flour

DIRECTIONS

1. In a large bowl with a hand mixer, beat the butter until light and fluffy. Add sugar, vanilla and salt and beat until combined.

2. Stir in the almond flour slowly until there are no more dry spots and add the chocolate chips. Cover the bowl with plastic wrap and place in the refrigerator to set, 15 to 20 minutes.

3. Use a small cookie scoop to scoop the dough into small balls. Store in the refrigerator if you plan to eat within a week, or in the freezer for up to 1 month.

27. Keto Cheese Bread For Women

YIELD: Makes one loaf |MIXING TIME: 10 mins |RISING TIME: About 45 mins |BAKING: 375°F for about 45 mins

INGREDIENTS:

- Unsalted butter for pan
- 1 cup whole milk
- 2¾ cups unbleached all-purpose flour
- 1 tbsp. granulated sugar
- ½ tsp. kosher salt
- 2¼ tsp. instant yeast (one ¼-oz packet)
- One egg
- 8 oz. sharp Cheddar cheese, cut into ½-to ¾-in pieces

DIRECTIONS:

1. Butter a 9-by-5-by-3-in loaf pan (or another loaf pan with an 8-cup capacity). Line the bottom of the pan with parchment paper.

2. In a saucepan, heat the milk overheats to about 130°F on an instant-read thermometer. Remove from the heat.

3. In a stand blender fitted with the flat beater, mix 1 cup of the flour, sugar, salt, and yeast on low speed until combined. Add the hot milk and mix until smoothly combined. Add the egg and continue beating for 2 mins. Add the remaining 1¾ cups flour and continue mixing for 5 mins. The dough will be soft and will come away from the sides of the bowl, and if you stop the blender and stick a finger into the dough, your finger will come out clean.

4. . Sprinkle the cheese pieces evenly over the top. Using the heel of one hand, push the dough down and away against the surface. Then, using your fingertips, fold it toward you. Rotate the dough a quarter turn and repeat the pushing and folding about five times. Several pieces of cheese will poke out of the dough. This is fine. The dough will firm s as the cheese is worked into it. The loaf will not fill the pan.

5. Let the dough rise to within 1 in the pan's top, about 45 mins. When the dough has risen for 25 mins, preheat the oven to375°F.

6. Bake the bread until the top feels firm and is browned for about 45 mins. Let cool in the pan for 10 mins. Run a sharp knife around the pans inside edge to loosen the bread sides, and then turn the bread out onto the rack. Let cool completely.

7. The bread can be stored in a plastic bag at room temperature for up to 3 days.

28. Crab And Zucchini Casserole

INGREDIENTS:

- 100 g crab meat
- ½ cup of sliced zucchini
- 4 asparagus
- 1 teaspoon of olive oil
- 1 sprig of fresh rosemary
- ½ cup of shredded cheddar cheese
- 1 clove of crushed garlic
- Salt and pepper

DIRECTIONS:

1. Blanch the zucchini and asparagus in a cooking pot. Add olive oil, rosemary, and garlic in a skillet. Fry until the garlic turns brown. Add the crabmeat, salt, and pepper—Cook for about 2 minutes. In an oven dish, first, add the zucchini and then a layer of crab meat. Then put the asparagus on top. Add the grated cheddar cheese to the asparagus and bake at 180 degrees C for 20-30 minutes.

29. Keto Avocado Pops

CAL / SERV: 120YIELD: 10PREP TIME:

0 HOURS 5 MIN TOTAL TIME: 6 HOURS 10 MIN

INGREDIENTS:

- 3 ripe avocados Juice of 2 limes (about 1/3 cup)
- 3 tablespoons. Swerve or other sugar alternative
- 3/4 c. coconut milk
- 1 tbsp. coconut oil
- 1 c. Keto-friendly chocolate

DIRECTIONS

1. Combine avocados in a blender or food processor with lime juice, Swerve and coconut milk. Mix until smooth and pour into the Popsicle mold.

2. Freeze until firm, 6 hours to overnight.

3. Combine chocolate chips and coconut oil in a medium bowl. Microwave until melted and let cool to room temperature. Dip frozen pops in chocolate and serve.

30. Bacon Pineapple Shrimp Skewers

Start to finish: 35 minutes Servings: 3 (for 6 large skewers)

INGREDIENTS:

- 18 medium or large wild caught shrimp
- 9 slices of uncured meadow bacon, cut in half and precooked (but still pliable)
- 1 1/2 cups organic pineapple chunks (24 pieces)
- 2 tablespoons grass-fed butter melted
- 1 teaspoon of dried oregano
- 3/4 teaspoon flaky sea salt
- Optional: fresh parsley for garnish

DIRECTIONS:

1. Preheat the grill over medium heat.

2. Wrap each shrimp with a piece of partially cooked bacon and set aside.

3. Assemble Shrimp Skewers: Alternate pineapple chunks with bacon-wrapped shrimp on each skewer. You should have 6 skewers, each with 3 shrimp and 4 pieces of pineapple. Put aside.

4. In a small bowl, combine melted butter or ghee, dried oregano, and flaky sea salt. Generously brush each shrimp skewer, front and back, with butter mixture.

5. Grill for about 2 minutes on each side or until shrimp are opaque and cooked through. Brush with more butter, garnish with chopped parsley, if desired, and serve.

31. Keto Stir-fried chicken

INGREDIENTS:

- 75 g chicken
- 1 clove of garlic
- ½ cup of bamboo shoots
- 1 tablespoon of butter
- 1 tablespoon of olive oil
- 1 dried red chili
- Chives
- Salt and pepper

DIRECTIONS:

1. Heat olive oil in a frying pan. Add the garlic and cook until it turns brown. Add the dried red chili and bamboo shoots and cook for about 3 minutes. Add the chicken, salt, and pepper. Stir and cook until the chicken is about 7 minutes. Toss in the chives and cook for 2 more minutes. Add the butter and let it sizzle for 1 minute. Place the chicken and bamboo shoots.

32. Grilled Salmon With Broccoli

INGREDIENTS:

- 100 g salmon fillet
- ½ cup of broccoli
- 2 teaspoons of butter
- ½ teaspoon of dried rosemary
- ½ teaspoon of dried thyme
- ½ teaspoon of garlic oil
- 2 tablespoons of mayonnaise with chili oil
- Salt and pepper

DIRECTIONS:

1. Mix 1 dried rosemary, dried thyme, and 1 teaspoon of butter, garlic oil, salt, and pepper in a bowl. Rub it over the salmon fillet. Preheat the grill and grill the salmon and broccoli for 6-7 minutes. Add 1 teaspoon of butter to the salmon. Sprinkle the broccoli with salt and pepper. Serve the grilled salmon and broccoli with mayonnaise-chili oil dip.

33. Grilled Flank Steak with Lemon Herb Sauce

PREP: 1 HOUR 30 MIN | COOKING: 30 MIN |
TOTAL: 2 HOURS | Servings 6

INGREDIENTS:

- 1½ pounds of flank steak
- ⅓ cup of olive oil
- ¼ cup of Worcestershire sauce
- ¼ cup of malt vinegar
- 3-cloves of garlic smashed
- 2-teaspoons chili powder
- 1-tablespoon of dried herbs (such as tarragon, thyme, or oregano, or a combination)
- Salt and freshly ground black pepper
- LEMON HERB SAUCE
- ⅓ cup of olive oil
- 3-anchovies, crushed into a paste

- 1-clove of garlic, finely chopped
- 1-tablespoon of whole-grain mustard
- 2-lemons, grated and squeezed
- ¾ cup of chopped fresh parsley
- ½ cup of freshly chopped basil
- ¼ cup of chopped fresh mint
- Salt and freshly ground black pepper

DIRECTIONS:

1. PREPARE THE STEAK: Place the flank steak in a large plastic zip-lock bag. In a medium bowl, whisk the oil with the Worcestershire sauce, vinegar, garlic, chili powder, and spices to combine. Pour the mixture over the steak and seal the bag. Marinate, chilled, for up to 1 hour.

2. MAKE THE SAUCE DURING THE STEAK MARINATES: Beat together the oil with the anchovies, garlic, mustard, lemon zest, and lemon juice. Stir in the herbs and season with salt and pepper.

3. When the steak is done marinating, remove it from the bag and wipe off the excess marinade—season with salt and pepper.

4. GRILL THE STEAK: Cook the steak on a hot grill (or grill pan) until well browned on the outside and at the desired doneness, about 5 to 7 minutes per side for medium-rare.

5. Remove the steak from the grill and let rest for 15 minutes. Slice the steak and serve immediately with the sauce.

34. Baked Salmon With Creamy Dill Sauce - Keto and Low Carb

INGREDIENTS:

- 6-pieces of fresh salmon (about 2" wide / 4 ounces each)
- 1-tablespoon of fresh dill, chopped
- Olive oil
- Salt and pepper to taste
- For the sauce
- 1-tablespoon of fresh dill, chopped
- ⅓ cup of sour cream
- 2-tablespoons of mayonnaise
- 1-teaspoon of Dijon mustard
- 1-tablespoon capers, chopped
- Juice and zest of ½ lemon
- Salt and pepper to taste

DIRECTIONS:

1. To make the sauce
2. Mix all sauces in a bowl and let them come to room temperature while you make the salmon.
3. To make the salmon
4. Preheat the oven to 400F.
5. Place the salmon on a wire rack, on a baking tray lined with aluminum foil (for easier cleaning). Brush each piece with olive oil. Sprinkle with salt, pepper, and dill.
6. Bake for 10 minutes.
7. Increase the temperature to 450F and bake for an additional 5-8 minutes.
8. Serve with a healthy dollop of sauce over the salmon and garnish with some dill and capers.

35. Keto Cauliflower bread

Time: 25 MINUTES Cooking time: 50 MINUTES

Total time: 1 HOUR 15 MINUTES

INGREDIENTS:

- 6-tablespoons canola oil (use olive oil if making paleo or Keto)
- 1 tbsp. baking powder
- 1-¼ cup of superfine almond flour
- 3 cups of cauliflower finely chopped
- 6-large eggs separated
- 1 tsp. salt

DIRECTIONS:

1. Firstly cook cauliflower for 3-4 minutes or until tender. Let the cauliflower cool. Once cooled, put a small amount in a tea towel and wring dry. Repeat with the remaining cauliflower, working in small batches.

2. Add egg whites to a mixing bowl. Beat at high speed until stiff peaks form. Put aside.

3. In a large bowl, combine egg yolks, oil, almond flour, baking powder, and salt. Mix until smooth paste forms. Stir in the cauliflower until evenly blended.

4. Add about 1/4 of the egg whites to the pasta. Use a spatula to fold in the egg whites. When the egg whites are completely collapsed, add another batch of egg whites and repeat until all of the egg whites have been processed. The mixture should look pale and fluffy. Be careful not to beat the egg whites as they will lose the air that is whipped in, and the bread will not rise properly.

5. Pour the batter into the prepared bread machine. Adjust the program of bread machine. Bake for about 45-50 minutes, or until bread is cooked through. Let the bread cool before slicing.

36. Chicken Meatballs and Cauliflower Rice with Coconut Herb Sauce

PREP: 25 MIN | COOKING: 20 MIN | TOTAL: 45 MIN | Servings 4

INGREDIENTS:

- MEATBALLS
- Non-stick spray
- 1-tablespoon of extra virgin olive oil
- ½ red onion
- 2-cloves of garlic, chopped
- 1 pound of ground chicken
- ¼ cup of chopped fresh parsley
- 1-tablespoon of Dijon mustard
- ¾ teaspoon of kosher salt
- ½ teaspoon of freshly ground black pepper

SAUCE

- A 14-ounce of coconut milk
- 1¼ cups of chopped fresh parsley, divided
- 4-spring onions, roughly chopped
- 1-clove of garlic, peeled and crushed
- Peel and juice one lemon
- Kosher salt and freshly ground black pepper
- Red pepper flakes, to serve
- One recipe Cauliflower rice

DIRECTIONS:

1. MAKE THE MEATBALLS: Preheat oven to 375 ° F. Line a baking tray with aluminum foil and spray with nonstick cooking spray.

2. In a medium skillet, heat the olive oil over medium heat. Add the onion and sauté until tender, about 5 minutes. Add the garlic and sauté until fragrant, about 1 minute.

3. Transfer the onion and garlic to a medium bowl and allow cooling slightly. Stir in chicken, parsley, and mustard; Season with salt and pepper. Shape the mixture into two tablespoons large balls and place on the baking tray.

4. Fry the meatballs until firm and cooked for 17 to 20 minutes.

5. MAKE THE SAUCE: In the bowl of a food processor, combine the coconut milk, parsley, spring onions, garlic, lemon zest, and lemon juice and mix until smooth; Season with salt and pepper.

6. Sprinkle the meatballs with the red pepper flakes and the rest of the parsley. Serve over the cauliflower rice with the sauce.

37. Keto yogurt bark recipe

INGREDIENTS:

- 1 cup of your favorite Keto yogurt
- 3 to 5 drops of liquid stevia or one tablespoon of your favorite powdered Keto sweetener to sweeten it to your liking
- 1/2 cup diced berries, strawberries, blueberries, blackberries, raspberries, etc.
- 1-teaspoon of vanilla extract

DIRECTIONS:

1. Mix the Keto yogurt with the sweetener, vanilla extract, and cinnamon (if using).
2. Place a piece of parchment paper on a baking tray or a large plate.
3. Divide the sweetened Keto yogurt over the baking paper.
4. Cut the berries into small bite-sized pieces.
5. Sprinkle the berries over the Keto yogurt.
6. Freeze for at least 3 hours or overnight.
7. Break the yogurt bark into bite-sized pieces.

38. Low-carb, baked kale, and broccoli salad

Time 10 + 20 + 3 minutes | Servings 2

INGREDIENTS:

- Broccoli florets
- Bare minced meat

DIRECTIONS:

1. Set aside.
2. (2.5 cm) higher than
3. The eggs. Cover and bring to a boil over high heat. Cook once, remove from
4. heat and boil in water, depending on preference: 10-12 minutes (hard-
5. Cooked), or 6-8 minutes (medium cooked), or 5-6 minutes (soft boiled).
6. Meanwhile, set aside a bowl of ice-cold water.

7. To peel. Peel under running water and cut into halves or quarters. Set

8. Aside.

9. Add the sliced garlic and fry until golden brown. Remove the garlic from the pan and place it on kitchen paper too crispy. Keep the garlic-infused oil in the pan.

10. With the olive oil. Add the broccoli, kale, and spring onions. Use pliers, throw to

11. Coat and bake for about 5 minutes, or until lightly cooked.

12. Board with the eggs, avocado, and mustard mayonnaise.

39. Low-carb asparagus salad with walnuts

INGREDIENTS:

- Fresh mint, for decoration

DIRECTIONS:

1. Minutes, or until light golden brown
2. the bottom ends, which are quite stringy and chewy
3. Then cut the remaining asparagus into thin, sloping asparagus slices.
4. Add the hot chili flakes, salt, and avocado
5. Oil and olive oil.
6. Mix the beat gently but well with a rubber spatula.

40. Low carbohydrate vegan bowl

INGREDIENTS:

- Spicy marinated tofu
- Firm tofu cut into 1-inch cubes
- Buddha bowl
- Mushrooms, sliced
- Cauliflower, cut into florets
- Broccoli, cut into small florets
- Baby bok choy

DIRECTIONS:

1. Spicy marinated tofu
2. Mixing
3. Well until all of the tofu is evenly coated.
4. Line a large baking dish with parchment paper
5. And divide the tofu into a single layer.
6. Buddha bowl
7. Set the mushrooms aside.
8. Toss in the cauliflower rice
9. The pan along with the chopped parsley and cook until soft, approx. For 10 minutes.
10. Microwave on high heat, approx. 5 minutes.
11. Add a splash of boiling water
12. To a medium skillet and place the bok choy in it, cut side down. Cook for 3-5
13. Minutes on low heat until just cooked and tender.
14. Place the
15. Broccoli and bok choy on the other side. Top with fried mushrooms and
16. Crispy marinated tofu. Garnish with sesame seeds and chili, if desired. Salt and
17. Pepper to taste.

41. Keto Breakfast Parfait Recipe - Low-carb yogurt, muesli, and berries

Prep Time: 10 minutes Cooking Time: 0 minutes Total Time: 10 minutes Servings: 2 servings

INGREDIENTS:

- ½ cup of Greek yogurt full of fat
- ¼ cup of heavy cream
- One teaspoon Vanilla Essence
- ½ cup of Keto Chocolate Almond Clusters
- Two strawberries cut into cubes
- Eight blueberries

DIRECTIONS:

1. In a mixing bowl, add the yogurt, cream, and vanilla. Beat until thick and smooth.

2. Spoon half of the yogurt between two glasses and then sprinkle half of the granola over it.

3. Add the remaining yogurt, followed by the remaining granola.

4. Cover with the berries and enjoy!

42. Keto Breakfast Parfait

INGREDIENTS:

- cups of Greek yogurt, whole milk
- 0.5 cup of heavy whipping cream
- 6-tablespoons of almond butter
- 2-teaspoons vanilla extract
- 1/2 cup of berries (raspberries and blueberries)
- 4-tablespoons of pecans, sliced
- 2-teaspoons of coconut flakes
- Fresh mint leaves, peeled, for garnish
- Cocoa powder, for garnish

DIRECTIONS:

1. Grab four individual containers of your choice and place them in a prep area. In a bowl, mix the Greek yogurt and whipped cream until fully incorporated. Divide 1/2 cup of Greek yogurt, mix into each container and press down with a spatula to flatten the surface of the yogurt. Then add 1.5 tablespoons of almond butter (or nut butter of your choice), either in the center as a dollop or vertically across the container. You're about to make an Instagram-worthy Keto breakfast parfait.

2. Then add 1/2 teaspoon of vanilla extract to each container, 1/8 cup of your desired berry mix (I love raspberries and blueberries) around the container. Top with 1/4 teaspoon of coconut flakes, one tablespoon of sliced pecans, and top with 1/4 teaspoon of coconut flakes. Garnish by gently sprinkling the cocoa powder over the parfait and adding freshly picked mint leaves.

43. Low Carb Turkey and Pepper

INGREDIENTS:

- 1 teaspoon of salt, divided
- 1 pound turkey fillet, cut into thin steaks of about ¼ inch thick sliced
- 2 tablespoons of extra virgin olive oil, divided
- ½ large sweet onion, sliced
- 1 red pepper, cut into strips
- 1 yellow pepper, cut into strips
- ½ teaspoon of Italian herbs
- ¼ teaspoon ground black pepper
- 2 teaspoons of red wine vinegar
- 1 14-ounce tomato, preferably fire-roasted
- Chopped fresh parsley and basil for garnish (optional)

DIRECTIONS:

1. Sprinkle ½ teaspoon of salt over turkey—heat 1 tablespoon of oil in a large non-stick frying pan over medium heat. Add half of the turkey and cook until brown on the bottom, 1 to 3 minutes. Flip and continue to cook until completely cooked 1 to 2 minutes. Place the turkey on a plate with a slotted spatula, tent with foil to keep warm. Add the remaining 1 tablespoon of oil to the pan, reduce the heat to medium and repeat with the remaining turkey, 1 to 3 minutes per side.

2. Add onion, bell pepper, and remaining ½ teaspoon of salt to the pan, cover, and cook, removing the lid to stir often until onion and bell pepper turn soft and blotchy brown, 5 to 7 minutes. Remove lid, increase heat to medium-low, drizzle with Italian herbs and pepper, and cook, often stirring, until spices are fragrant, about 30 seconds. Add vinegar and cook, stirring until almost completely evaporated, about 20 seconds. Add tomatoes and bring to a boil, stirring frequently.

3. Add the turkey to the pan with any accumulated juices from the plate and bring it to a boil. Reduce heat to medium-low and cook, turning sauce over until turkey is completely hot, 1 to 2 minutes. Serve with parsley and basil if desired.

44. Keto Butter Chicken

INGREDIENTS:

- lbs. of chicken breast cut into cubes
- 2 tablespoons of garam masala
- 3 teaspoons fresh ginger grated
- 3 teaspoons of minced garlic
- 4 oz. whole milk Greek yogurt
- 1 tablespoon of coconut oil
- *Sauce:*
- 2 tablespoons of ghee or butter
- 1 onion
- 2 teaspoons of fresh ginger grated
- 2 teaspoons of chopped garlic
- 14.5 oz. can have crushed tomatoes
- 1 tablespoon of ground coriander
- ½ tablespoon of garam masala
- 2 teaspoons of cumin

- 1 teaspoon chili powder
- ½ cup of whipped cream
- Salt to taste
- Optional for serving:
- Chopped cilantro
- Cauliflower rice
- Sliced fresh jalapeños

DIRECTIONS:

1. Cut the chicken into 5 cm pieces and place in a large bowl with 2 tablespoons of garam masala, 1 teaspoon of grated ginger, and 1 teaspoon of chopped garlic. Add the yogurt, stir to combine. Transfer to the refrigerator and refrigerate for at least 30 minutes.

2. For the sauce, put the onion, ginger, garlic, crushed tomatoes, and herbs in a blender and blend until smooth. Put aside—heat 1 tablespoon of oil in a large skillet over medium heat. Place the chicken in the pan along with the marinade and brown for 3 to 4 minutes per side. Once browned, pour the sauce and cook for 5 to 6 minutes longer.

3. Stir in the whipped cream and ghee and cook for another minute. Taste for salt and add extra if necessary. Finish with cilantro and serve with cauliflower rice if desired.

45. Keto fried bacon omelet

Preparation Time: 5 Mins | Cooking Time: 20 Mins | Portions 2

INGREDIENTS:

- 4 eggs
- 5 oz. bacon cut into cubes
- 3 oz. butter
- 2 ounces fresh spinach
- 1 tablespoon finely chopped fresh chives (optional)
- Salt and pepper

DIRECTIONS:

1. Preheat the oven to 400 ° F (200 ° C). Grease an individual baking dish with butter.

2. Fry bacon and spinach in the remaining butter.

3. Beat the eggs until frothy. Mix in the spinach and bacon, including the fat leftover from frying. Add some finely chopped chives. Season with Salt and Pepper.

4. Pour the egg mixture into the baking dish (s) and bake for 20 minutes or until firm and golden brown.

5. Let cool for a few minutes and serve.

46. Keto chicken wings with creamy broccoli

Preparation Time: 10 Mins | Cooking Time: 45 Mins | Portions 2

INGREDIENTS:

- Fried chicken wings
- ½ orange, juice, and zest
- ¼ cup of olive oil
- 2 tsp. ginger powder
- 1 teaspoon of salt
- ¼ tsp. cayenne pepper
- 3 lbs. chicken wings
- Creamy broccoli
- 1½ pounds of broccoli
- 1 cup of mayonnaise
- ¼ cup of chopped fresh dill
- Salt and pepper, to taste

DIRECTIONS:

1. Preheat the oven to 400 ° F (200 ° C). In a small bowl, mix juice and zest of the orange with oil and spices. Place the chicken wings in a plastic bag and add the marinade. Shake the bag well to cover the wings well.

2. Set aside to marinate for at least 5 minutes, but preferably longer. Place the wings in one layer in a greased baking dish or on a grill rack for extra crunchiness.

3. Bake on the middle rack in the oven for about 45 minutes or until the wings are golden and well cooked. In the meantime, divide the broccoli into small florets and boil them in salted water for a few minutes.

4. They should only soften a little but do not lose their shape or color. Strain the broccoli and let some of the steam evaporate before adding the remaining ingredients. Serve the broccoli with the fried wings.

47. Keto chicken thighs with mozzarella cheese

Preparation time: 10 minutes Cooking time: 30 minutes Total time: 40 Yield: 6

INGREDIENTS:

- 3 tablespoons of extra virgin olive oil, divided
- 2 lbs. boneless chicken thighs
- 1½ tablespoons of Italian herbs, divided
- Sea salt and black pepper, to taste
- 3 tablespoons butter (unsalted is better for you, but salted works too)
- ¼ cup of chicken stock, preferably organic
- ½ c. Multicolored cherry tomatoes, quartered or sliced tomatoes (the quartered cherry tomatoes are low key there for visual appeal - so use what you have :)

- 8 oz. Fresh mozzarella cheese, sliced or use 1 cup shredded - tried both ways, and I enjoy both
- ½ teaspoon of red pepper flakes

DIRECTIONS:

1. Preheat the oven to 425 ° F.
2. First, heat 1 tablespoon of olive oil in a large, oven-proof skillet over medium heat.
3. Then brush the chicken thighs with the other 2 tablespoons of olive oil and sprinkle both sides with a tablespoon of Italian herbs. Add salt and pepper - to taste. Then move everything to an ovenproof skillet
4. Cook the chicken for 4-5 minutes on each side, or until the chicken has a golden-brown crust and you can't stand it anymore. Remove from heat and add butter, chicken stock and cherry tomatoes. Cover each chicken thigh with a slice of fresh mozzarella cheese (or shredded) and sprinkle with crushed red pepper flakes and the remaining Italian seasoning.

5. Then transfer the skillet to the preheated oven and roast for 15-20 minutes, or until the chicken is cooked through and the mozzarella has melted. Remove from oven and let the chicken cool for 5 minutes.

6. To serve, top chicken with some pan sauce and fresh basil sprigs, if desired. Serve immediately with loaded cauliflower for a complete Keto dinner meal or a side dish of your choice.

7. To enjoy!

48. Steaks With Mushroom Sauce

10 minutes | COOKING TIME 15 minutes |
TOTAL TIME 25 minutes

INGREDIENTS:

FOR THE FILLET:

- 2 steaks of filet mignon
- 2 tbsp. avocado oil
- Kosher salt
- Freshly cracked black pepper

FOR THE SAUCE:

- 2 cups of baby Bella mushrooms, thinly sliced
- 1/4 cup yellow onion, finely chopped
- 1 tsp. fresh thyme leaves
- Two cloves of garlic, chopped
- Kosher salt (to taste)

- Freshly cracked black pepper (to taste)
- 1/4 cup beef stock
- 2 tbsp. balsamic vinegar

DIRECTIONS:

1. For the fillet:
2. Pat the steaks dry with kitchen paper until they are as dry as possible throughout [this will give your steak a better crust]. Generously season both sides of the steaks with kosher salt and cracked black pepper.
3. Heat a cast-iron skillet over medium heat for 4 minutes without touching it. Add the oil to the pan when it is hot. When the oil just starts to smoke, you are ready to cook your steaks. You want to make sure the skillet is super-hot.
4. Carefully place the fillets in the pan and cook until golden brown on both sides and cooked to your liking, depending on the size of your steaks and how you want yours cooked. My fillets were on the small side, and I cooked mine for 2-3 minutes on each side for medium / medium-rare cook.
5. Transfer the cooked steaks to a plate and let them rest while you make the mushroom sauce.

6. For the sauce:

7. Add the onion and garlic and cook, stirring, for about 2 minutes until the onions are slightly tender.

8. Add the mushrooms with a pinch of salt and pepper and continue cooking, stirring, to brown the mushrooms slightly, about 3 minutes. When the mushrooms soften, add the thyme, beef stock, and balsamic vinegar and stir to combine.

9. Continue cooking, stir-fry, until sauce is reduced by about half, 3 to 4 minutes.

49. Carb Keto Cheese Sauce Recipe

Cooking time5 minutes | Total time 5 minutes | Servings 8

INGREDIENTS:

- 2 cups cheddar cheese (shredded)
- 1/4 cup of heavy cream
- Two tablespoons unsweetened almond milk (or milk of your choice, or more cream)
- One tablespoon butter (optional, but recommended for a richer sauce)

DIRECTIONS:

1. Combine all in a saucepan over low heat. Heat, stirring regularly until the cheese mixture is smooth. Be careful not to overheat, or the cheese will burn.

50. Zucchini Pizza Crust

Preparation Time: 15 mins |Cooking Time: 30 mins |Total Time: 45 mins | For 8 slices

INGREDIENTS:

- 8 oz. Zucchini (about 2 cups coarsely grated, loosely packed in the measuring cup)
- 3 large eggs
- 1 cup mozzarella cheese (shredded; use pre-cut or hard block mozzarella, * not * soft fresh)
- 1/4 cup Healthy Yum Coconut Flour
- 1/2 teaspoon sea salt (plus a little more for sprinkling in Step 2)
- Keto flour

DIRECTIONS:

1. Preheat the oven to 350 degrees F (177 degrees C). Grease a 12- or 14-inch non-stick pizza plate. (30 or 36 cm) (Use parchment paper if it is not an excellent non-stick coating.)

2. Spread the grated zucchini in a thin layer over the pan. Sprinkle very lightly with a little sea salt (not 1/2 teaspoon, this is just a light sprinkle). Bake for about 10-15 minutes, until the zucchini is semi-soft and moderately dry.

3. Meanwhile, combine the eggs, mozzarella, coconut flour, and 1/2 teaspoon of sea salt in a large bowl.

4. When the zucchini is cooked, pat them dry with kitchen paper as best you can. Mix in the bowl.

5. Lightly wipe the pizza plate to remove any stuck zucchini. If it's not a very good non-stick coating, line with parchment paper. Grease the pan or baking paper.

6. Divide the zucchini pizza dough into a thin circle about 11-12 in (28-30 cm) in diameter. Bake for 20-30 minutes, until brown spots appear on top. (The time will depend on the thickness of the zucchini pizza base.)

7. Remove the zucchini pizza base from the oven. Increase the oven temperature to 400 degrees F (204 degrees C) and let it preheat.

8. Let the crust rest at room temperature for 10 minutes and cover with thick sauce and toppings.

9. Return the zucchini crust pizza to the oven for about 10 minutes, until the cheese melts on top. If desired, place under the broiler for a few minutes to brown the cheese.

Conclusion

I would like to thank you for choosing this book. All the recipes in this book are very beneficial for women and contain less carbs. These recipes are more delicious and rich in nutrients. You must try at home and appreciate.
I wish you all good luck!

KETO COOKBOOK FOR MEN

Table of Contents

Introduction ------------------------------------**139**

Keto Meal Recipes For Men --------------------**140**

40+ Recipes------------------------------------**140**

1. Keto Eggplant Moussaka Recipe ------------ 140
2. Keto Shepherd's Pie ------------------------ 143
3. Keto Instant Pot Bolognese ---------------- 145
4. Low-Carb Cabbage Cake Recipe ------------ 148
5. Keto Keema Curry -------------------------- 151
6. Low-Carb Bourguignon Stew --------------- 154
7. Cheesy Keto Meatball Casserole ------------ 160
8. Keto Beef Meal ----------------------------- 163
9. Keto Beef And Broccoli -------------------- 168
10. Keto Easy Meatballs ----------------------- 170
11. Keto Mongolian Beef----------------------- 173
12. Easy Keto Burger -------------------------- 176
13. Keto Curry Bowl With Spinach ------------- 180
14. Keto Chili Recipe -------------------------- 182
15. Ground Beef Stroganoff -------------------- 184
16. Lamb & Beef Balti------------------------- 186
17. Keto Stuffed Pepper Recipe ---------------- 188
18. Beef Liver With Bacon Recipe -------------- 190
19. Keto Burrito Peppers----------------------- 193

20. Keto Meat Pie-------------------------------- 196

21. Easy Pork Crawler Recipe With Vegetables (Low Carb) --------------------------------------- 199

22. Keto Stuffed Pork Tenderloin With Mushroom Sauce--- 203

23. Keto Short Ribs Recipe --------------------- 206

24. Easy Cheesy Low Carb Keto Spinach Artichoke Dip Recipe ---------------------------------- 209

25. Keto Stuffed Meatballs Cheese------------- 212

26. Keto Asparagus Fries ---------------------- 215

27. Keto Stuffed Mushrooms With Sausage ---- 217

28. Shrimp Rangoon Mini Paprika -------------- 219

29. Smoked Trout Mousse ---------------------- 222

30. Crack Dip Recipe With Bacon And Cream Cheese --- 224

31. Baked Salami Mozzarella Bites------------- 226

32. Keto Shrimp Guacamole And Bacon -------- 228

33. Keto Chips With Sour Cream And Onion --- 231

Conclusion -----------------------------------**234**

INTRODUCTION

A ketogenic diet is made chiefly out of calories from fat and just few calories from starches. The diet powers the body to devour fat rather than carbs for energy. When in doubt, the starches you eat are changed over into glucose in the body, used to the energy around the body and in the mind. In any case, in the event that you neglected to eat enough sugars, your body will utilize a crisis framework to consume fat. The EU can eat the put away fat and fat you eat for energy. The put away fat is separated into two sections, the fattest acids, and the ketone bodies. The keton bodies bring the cerebrum's energy rather than glucose. This state of numerous ketone bodies in your blood is called ketosis. This book contains ketogenic meals recipes for men which carry huge benefits regarding health.

Keto meal recipes for men
40+ recipes

1. Keto Eggplant Moussaka Recipe

Preparation Time: 10 mins |Cooking Time: 1 hour| Total Time: 1 hour 10 mins

INGREDIENTS:

- 2 Aubergine - cut into 1/2 cm rounds
- 3 tbsp. olive oil
- 1 1/2 lb. lean ground beef or meatloaf mix
- 1 onion - small, chopped
- 2 cloves of garlic - pressed
- 1 cup of tomato sauce
- 1/2 cup vegetable or beef stock - can be replaced with dry white wine

- 3 tbsp. parsley - chopped, fresh
- 3 tablespoons of breadcrumbs - ground pork rinds for Keto
- 2 proteins
- 1 tsp. salt
- 1/2 teaspoon of black pepper

DIRECTIONS:

1. Preheat the oven to 375F. Divide the eggplant rounds over one or two frying pans. Brush with olive oil. Bake for 10 minutes, until soft and slightly dried. Let them cool down.
2. In the meantime, prepare the meat sauce. Heat the remaining olive oil in a frying pan, add the meat and cook until the meat is no longer pink and becomes crumbly. Add the onion and garlic. Cook on medium for 5 minutes.

3. Add the tomato sauce and stock (or wine)—season with salt and pepper. Bring to a boil and reduce heat to low. Simmer for 15 minutes. Remove from heat and let the sauce cool for 10 minutes. Mix in the breadcrumbs (pork rinds for Keto) and the egg whites. Add parsley.

4. Grease a 9x13 inch baking dish (or any other dish closer to these dimensions). Layer 1/2 of the eggplant rounds. Add the minced meat sauce. Finish with the remaining eggplant rounds.

5. Combine butter, milk, and cornstarch in a saucepan. Bring to a boil, constantly whisking until the mixture thickens. Reduce heat and simmer for 2 minutes. Stir in half of the cheese. Add ground nutmeg, 1/8 tsp. black pepper, and 1/2 tsp. salt. Pour over the dish, cover with the rest of the cheese and bake at 350 degrees for 40-50 minutes until golden brown.

6. Heat whipped cream, then add butter and 1 cup of cheese, stir until melted. Add salt, pepper to taste, and nutmeg.

2. Keto Shepherd's Pie

Preparation Time: 30 min |Cooking Time: 30 min | Servings: 8 | Calories per Serving: 350kcal

INGREDIENTS:

- Filling
- Cauliflower Topping

DIRECTIONS:

1. Heat oil in a large saucepan over medium heat. Add beef (or Lamb) and cook until no longer pink, dividing with a wooden spoon and stirring frequently, about 5 minutes.

2. Add diced onions, celery, carrots, garlic and herbs to the pan. Cook until vegetables soften, about 5 minutes, stirring occasionally.

3. Add stock, tomato paste, and Worcestershire sauce to the pan and stir until the pasta has dissolved. Reduce the heat slightly and simmer for about 15 minutes until the sauce thickens, before turning off the heat.

4. Preheat the oven to 400 degrees F.

5. Place steamed cauliflower in a food processor or blender. Add ½ cup of cheddar cheese, cream cheese, cream, butter, garlic, salt and pepper. Puree to a smooth consistency and scrape the sides if necessary (see video above for steps on how to steam the cauliflower).

6. Transfer the meat and vegetable mixture to a 2-quart baking dish, dividing it into an even layer.

7. Divide the mashed cauliflower evenly over the meat and cover with the remaining shredded cheddar cheese.

8. Bake for 30 minutes, or until the tops of the mashed cauliflower are brown. Remove from oven and let cool slightly, then garnish with parsley, if desired. Serve immediately.

3. Keto Instant Pot Bolognese

Preparation Time: 10 mins

INGREDIENTS:

- 1 tbsp. olive oil
- 1/4-pound pancetta
- 1 pound ground beef
- 1 pound of ground pork
- 1 tbsp. tomato paste
- 1 tbsp. butter
- 1/2 onion
- 2 celery stalks chopped
- 2 cloves of garlic
- 1 c red wine
- 1/2 c beef stock or stock

- 2 bay leaves
- 1/4 c flat-leaf parsley
- 1/4 c heavy cream
- 1 pinch of nutmeg
- salt / pepper to taste

DIRECTIONS:

1. Heat olive oil in the Instant Pot on the hottest sauté setting. Add pancetta until fat has melted, about 5 minutes

2. Add minced meat and ground pork and tomato paste until brown.

3. Remove the meat from the instant pan with a slotted spoon and set it aside in a bowl.

4. Still on the high sauté setting, add 1 tablespoon of butter until melted. Toss in the onions, celery, and garlic. Cook until onions are soft, 8-10 minutes

5. Deglaze by adding a splash of red wine, scraping the brown bits from the bottom of the pan, then pour in the rest of the wine. Add the meat mixture, bay leaves and beef stock.

6. Place the lid on the instant jar, seal and run the unit on HIGH pressure for 20 minutes.

7. Use the quick relief valve to vent all steam. Uncover the pot and set the Instant Pot on the lowest setting for baking heat and bring to a bubble. Simmer uncovered for 10-15 minutes, stirring often, until the sauce is the desired consistency.

8. Turn off the heat. Stir in the fresh parsley, whipped cream and ground nutmeg. Season with salt and pepper.

4. Low-Carb Cabbage Cake Recipe

Preparation Time: 45 min |Cooking Time: 45 min | Total Time: 1 hour 30 min| Servings: 6

INGREDIENTS:

- 1 cup savoy cabbage (or green cabbage)
- 2 pounds of ground beef
- 1 onion (finely chopped)
- 1 red bell pepper (diced)
- 1 green pepper (diced)
- 4 cloves of garlic (finely chopped)
- 1 teaspoon of dried basil
- 1 tablespoon Worcestershire sauce
- 1 cup of grated Romano (or parmesan cheese)
- 1 cup of ricotta cheese

- 1/2 cup marinara sauce (plus extra for topping)
- 2 cups of grated mozzarella cheese
- 1 egg
- 2 tablespoons of olive oil
- 1 tablespoon fresh basil (chopped)
- 1 tablespoon fresh parsley (finely chopped)
- salt and pepper

DIRECTIONS:

1. Preheat the oven to 350 degrees F.
2. Core and separate the leaves from the cabbage, then cook them in boiling water for 5 minutes. Drain well, pat dry and set aside.
3. Grease the bottom and sides of a 23 cm spring form pan with olive oil and place the largest leaves on the bottom so that they cover the bottom and sides of the pan.
4. Place a large skillet over medium heat and break the meat and cook it with a wooden spoon until it is no longer pink, then drain the fat and set the meat aside.

5. Add the olive oil, add the onion, bell pepper, garlic, and dried basil once it is hot, then cook and stir until the vegetables are tender, about 5 minutes. Add the cooked meat and stir to combine. Season with salt and pepper.
6. Add Worcestershire sauce, grated parmesan, ricotta, marinara, fresh basil and parsley, cook for another 5-7 minutes, set aside, cool and mix in egg.
7. Add the first layer of meat mixture, add grated mozzarella cheese and layer a cabbage leaf on top to cover the meat mixture. Repeat until you reach the top or without filling.
8. Finish with cabbage leaves and put them all around in the dish.
9. Drizzle the top with a little olive oil, salt and pepper and some parmesan cheese.
10. Bake in the preheated oven for about 40-50 minutes.
11. Let it rest for 15-20 minutes and then remove the sides of the spring form pan.
12. Slice and serve with more heated marinara sauce, parsley and grated cheese.

5. Keto Keema Curry

Preparation Time: 10 mins |Cooking Time: 40 mins | Total Time: 50 mins| Yield for People: 4

INGREDIENTS:

- 450 g extra lean ground beef
- 1 large onion, finely chopped
- 1 large carrot, finely chopped
- 1 celery stalk, finely chopped
- 3 cloves of garlic, crushed
- 1 heaped teaspoon of freshly grated ginger
- 2 teaspoons of cumin seeds
- 2 teaspoons ground cilantro
- 1 teaspoon deggi mirch Chili Powder (can add more if you really like spicy).

- 1 teaspoon of garam masala
- 1 teaspoon of turmeric
- 1 cup of frozen peas
- 4 tablespoons of tomato paste
- 2.5 cups (600 ml) beef stock (use only 1.5 cups for instant pot)
- freshly chopped cilantro to serve
- salt and black pepper
- cooking oil spray (I used avocado)

DIRECTIONS:

Stove Top:

1. Spray a frying pan over medium heat with some spray oil
2. Add the onion, garlic, carrot, celery and ginger and cook for about 5 minutes to soften them.
3. Add the ground beef and cook until brown, breaking large pieces apart with the back of a wooden spoon while cooking.
4. Stir in all the spices (plus the green chilies if using) and tomato paste and mix until evenly coated.
5. Add the stock and bring to a boil, reduce the heat and simmer until the meat is cooked through and the stock has thickened - about 30 minutes

6. Stir in the peas for the last few minutes.

7. Taste and season with salt and black pepper.

8. Serve with freshly chopped cilantro and steamed rice.

Instant Pot:

1. Set instant pot bake mode

2. Add ground beef, onion, celery, carrot, garlic and ginger

3. Fry until the beef is brown.

4. Add all other (except peas and cilantro)

5. Switch to 12 minutes (high) and make sure the valve is closed.

6. When it beeps to indicate its done cooking, open the valve to release the pressure quickly.

7. Switch back to baking mode and simmer for about 1-2 minutes to heat through the peas.

8. Taste and season with salt and black pepper.

9. Serve with chopped fresh cilantro and your choice of side dishes.

6. Low-Carb Bourguignon Stew

Preparation Time: 30 min |Cooking Time: 30 min | Total Time: 1 hour| Servings: 6

INGREDIENTS:

- 4 slices of bacon Cut crosswise
- 1 1/2 pounds of stew meat cut into 1 1/2 - 2-inch cubes and dried with a paper towel
- 4 ounces white onion (about 1 small)
- 2 celery stalks sliced
- 8 ounces of mushrooms chopped thick
- 1 clove of garlic crushed
- 1/2 teaspoon of xanthan gum
- 1 cup of dry burgundy wine
- 1 cup beef stock (or low-salt broth)
- 2 tablespoons of tomato paste
- 1/2 teaspoon of dried thyme

- 1 bay leaf
- 1/2 teaspoon sea salt (or to taste)
- 1/4 teaspoon black pepper, freshly ground
- 1 tablespoon fresh chopped parsley

DIRECTIONS:

1. With the lid of the Instant Pot, choose the sauté setting. When the "hot" indications show, add the bacon. Cook the bacon, stirring occasionally, until crispy. Remove to a paper towel lined plate. Don't throw away bacon fat.

2. Add half of the beef to the Instant Pot. Lumps should not touch each other. Sprinkle with salt and pepper. Let the first side brown before turning it over. Brown all sides and place on a plate. Repeat for the other half of the meat. If the Instant Pot turns off during this process, set it back to Sauté.

3. Discard all but 1 tablespoon of dripping water from the jar. (If there is less than 1 tablespoon, preferably add about a tablespoon of butter or oil to the instant pan.) Continue with the sauté setting and add onion and celery to the pan. Cook until just starting to soften. Add mushrooms. Cook vegetables until the mushrooms soften. Stir in the garlic and cook for a minute. Transfer to a plate

4. When there is no more oil in the jar, add about a teaspoon. Add xanthan gum to the jar. Stir to distribute the oil through the xanthan gum. Pour in burgundy and stir, scrape brown pieces. Bring to a boil and simmer until the wine starts to thicken. Add beef stock. Stir in the tomato paste, thyme and bay leaf. Bring to boil. Simmer until the stock has thickened enough to cover a spoon. Return the browned chunks of beef (along with the drippings) and bacon to the pot. Stir in salt and pepper.

5. Cover the Instant Pot. Set the steam lever to "Sealing". Select the Meat / Stew function and press the +/- buttons to set the time to 30 minutes. When the stew is ready, use the Quick Release method (refer to the Instant Pot manual) to vent the Instant Pot. Press Cancel. Make sure the float valve is down before opening the lid.

6. Taste and adjust seasoning. Remove the bay leaf and sprinkle with parsley before serving.

7. Slow Cooker *DIRECTIONS:*: (Add 5 hours 30 minutes to the cooking time)

8. Heat a large stockpot or frying pan over medium heat. When the pan is hot, add the bacon. Cook the bacon, stirring occasionally, until crispy. Place on a paper towel-lined plate to drain and transfer to the slow cooker

9. Add half of the beef to the pan. Lumps should not touch each other. Sprinkle with salt and pepper. Let the first side brown before turning it over. Brown all sides and put them in the slow cooker. Repeat for the other half of the meat.

10. Discard all but 1 tablespoon of dripping water from the jar. If there is less than a tablespoon, add a little oil of your choice. Continue over medium heat and add onion and celery to the pan. Cook until just starting to soften. Add mushrooms. Cook vegetables until the mushrooms soften. Stir in the garlic and cook for a minute. Transfer vegetables to the crockpot.

11. When there is no more oil in the jar, add about a teaspoon of the oil of your choice. Add xanthan gum to the jar. Stir to distribute in the oil. Pour in burgundy and stir, scrape brown pieces. Bring to a boil and simmer until the wine starts to thicken. Add beef stock. Stir in the tomato paste, thyme and bay leaf. Bring to boil. Simmer until the stock has thickened enough to cover a spoon. Stir in salt and pepper. Transfer to the slow cooker and stir along with the bacon, beef, and vegetables.

12. Cover the slow cooker. Cook the stew on a low heat for 6-8 hours or until the meat falls apart and is cooked through.

13. Taste and adjust the spices before serving. Remove the bay leaf and sprinkle with parsley before serving.

7. Cheesy Keto Meatball Casserole

Preparation Time: 5 mins |Cooking Time: 40 mins | Total Time: 45 mins

INGREDIENTS:

For the meatballs:

- 2 pounds of ground beef
- 1/2 cup of grated Parmesan cheese
- 3/4 cup shredded mozzarella cheese
- 1 egg
- 1/4 cup of grated onion
- 3 cloves of garlic, chopped
- 3 tablespoons of chopped fresh parsley
- 1/2 teaspoon onion powder
- 1/2 teaspoon garlic powder

- 1/2 teaspoon of Italian seasoning
- Salt and pepper to taste

For the frying pan:

- 1 (24 oz.) jar of favorite marinara sauce (I prefer Rao's)
- 1/2 cup of ricotta cheese
- 1/2 cup of grated mozzarella cheese
- 2 to 3 tablespoons of fresh basil, chopped

DIRECTIONS:

1. Preheat the oven to 400 degrees F.
2. To make the meatballs: Combine ground beef, cheese, egg, onion, garlic, parsley and herbs in a large bowl and mix well. Use a cookie spoon to shape the meatballs so that they are all the same size, roll them around in your hands and place on a baking dish or baking tray. You should get about 15 to 16 large meatballs.
3. Bake meatballs for 20 to 25 minutes, or until cooked through. Remove meatballs, drain excess fat and place cooked meatballs in a baking dish.

4. Pour the marinara sauce evenly over the meatballs and spoon over the ricotta cheese. Sprinkle with mozzarella cheese and bake in the oven for about 15 minutes until the cheese is melted and bubbly.

5. Remove from oven and cover with fresh basil. Serve and enjoy!

8. Keto Beef Meal

Preparation Time: 15 mins |Cooking Time: 30 mins | Total Time: 45 mins| Servings: 5

INGREDIENTS:

- 2 pounds of ground beef
- 2 teaspoons fresh parsley and mint chopped
- 1.5 teaspoons smoked paprika and cumin
- ¼ teaspoon of cayenne pepper
- 2 cloves of garlic grated
- ½ teaspoon of dried thyme
- Peel ½ lemon
- Kosher salt and black pepper
- Avocado or grape seed oil

- ¾ cup of full-fat Greek yogurt
- 1 teaspoon fresh parsley and mint chopped
- Peel of half a lemon
- 1 tablespoon of lemon juice
- 1 clove of garlic
- 1 teaspoon of extra virgin olive oil
- Kosher salt and black pepper
- 2 medium zucchinis of about 12 grams
- ½ head of cauliflower
- 1 pound broccoli with stalks or 12 ounces florets
- ½ onion chopped
- 2 cloves of garlic finely chopped
- 1 teaspoon of mustard seeds
- ¼ teaspoon of red pepper flakes
- 1 teaspoon fresh parsley and mint chopped
- Peel and juice from half a lemon
- 2 tablespoons chopped pecans toasted if desired
- Kosher salt and black pepper
- Avocado or grape seed oil

DIRECTIONS:

1. Cook's notes: Watch the video in this post to learn how to cut the zucchini, cauliflower, and broccoli for the pilaf. Everything is cut small and similar in size, so they cook evenly.

2. Make the pilaf by chopping the zucchini, cauliflower, and broccoli into small pieces that are about the same size, being careful not to use too much of the stems. Preheat a large and wide pan over medium heat for 2 minutes. Add 2 teaspoons of oil to the pan, then the onions, garlic, mustard seeds, red pepper flakes, ¼ teaspoon of salt, and a few cracks of pepper.

3. Mix well and cook for 6 minutes, stirring often. Add the chopped zucchini, cauliflower, and broccoli to the pan along with ½ teaspoon of salt and a few cracks of pepper. Mix well and put a lid on the pan; you can also use a baking tray to cover the pan if you don't have a lid. Cook for 10-12 minutes, stirring a few times.

4. The vegetables are ready when they have softened but still have a bite. Reduce heat and add parsley, mint, lemon zest and juice, and pecans, tossing well. Check for herbs; you may need more lemon juice or salt. Put aside.

5. Add to rounds kefta the beef to a large bowl with the remaining (not oil), 1 teaspoon salt, and a few cracked peppers. Use your hands to mix everything very well. Shape the kefta by taking some of the meat and shaping it like a block of wood or football; watch the video to see how.

6. You have enough beef to 14-15 kefta make. Preheat a large pan, preferably cast iron, over medium heat for 2 minutes. Add 2 teaspoons of oil to the pan, wait 30 seconds for the oil to heat up, and then add half of the kefta to the pan. Cook for 3-4 minutes, or until well browned, flip and cook for another 3-4 minutes.

7. If both sides are brown, you may need to cook the kefta on the sides for 30 seconds to cook them all the way through. If you are not sure if the kefta is cooked, cut one in half and check that it is important not to overcook the kefta, or they will dry out.

8. Remove kefta from the pan, add a little more oil and cook the second batch. While the kefta is cooking, make the yogurt sauce by combining everything in a bowl and whipping well. Check for herbs and adjust if necessary.

9. Serve the kefta with some yogurt sauce and pilaf; enjoy! Everything will keep in the fridge for 5 days, you can freeze the kefta for 2-3 months, but I would not recommend freezing the vegetables as they become very soft and watery. The best way to kefta and vegetables to warm up, 10 minutes in an oven at 400 F; if you use a microwave, cover the container or with a wet paper towel and make sure it does not overheat because of the meat from drying out.

9. Keto Beef and Broccoli

Preparation Time: 10 mins |Cooking Time: 25 mins | Total Time: 35 mins| Calories: 294kcal

INGREDIENTS:

- 1 pound flank steak cut into 1/4-inch-thick strips
- 5 cups of small broccoli florets about 7 ounces
- 1 tablespoon of avocado oil
- 1 yellow onion sliced
- 1 tablespoon of butter
- ½ tbsp. olive oil
- 1/3 cup of low-sodium soy sauce
- ⅓ cup of beef stock
- 1 tablespoon of fresh ginger finely chopped
- 2 cloves of garlic finely chopped

DIRECTIONS:

1. Heat avocado oil in a pan over medium heat for a few minutes or until hot.

2. Add sliced beef and cook until brown, less than 5 minutes, don't stir too much, you want it to brown. Place on a plate and set aside.

3. Add onions to a skillet with butter and olive oil and cook for 20 minutes until onions are caramelized and tender.

4. Add all other sauce to the pan and stir the together over medium heat until it begins to simmer for about 5 minutes.

5. Use a hand blender to mix sauce.

6. Keep the sauce warm on low heat and add broccoli to the pan.

7. Return the beef to the pan and toss with the broccoli and sauce. Stir until covered with the sauce.

8. Bring to a boil and cook for a few more minutes until the broccoli is tender.

9. Season with salt and pepper, if necessary.

10. Serve immediately, possibly in combination with boiled cauliflower rice.

10.Keto easy Meatballs

Preparation Time: 40 mins |Cooking Time: 25 mins | Yield: 6 Servings

INGREDIENTS:

For the meatballs:

- 1 pound ground beef (80/20)
- 1 pound ground lamb
- 1/2 cup of super fine blanched almond flour
- 2 eggs
- 1 tablespoon of Worcestershire sauce
- 1 tablespoon of finely grated carrot
- 1 teaspoon of fresh thyme leaves
- 1/2 teaspoon garlic powder
- 1/2 teaspoon onion powder
- 2 teaspoons kosher salt
- 1/2 teaspoon ground black pepper

- 2 tablespoons of olive oil for frying

For the sauce:
- 1 tablespoon of tomato paste
- 1 1/2 tablespoons Worcestershire sauce
- 1 1/4 cups of chicken stock
- 1/2 teaspoon kosher salt
- 1/2 teaspoon mustard powder
- 1/4 teaspoon black pepper
- 1/4 teaspoon of xanthan gum

DIRECTIONS:

1. Place the entire meatball (except the oil) in a medium bowl. Mix well with your hands and then shape into 18 meatballs, about 5cm in diameter.
2. Heat the oil in a large nonstick skillet over medium heat for about 2 minutes, or until the oil is shimmering.
3. Add the meatballs and cook for about 3 minutes, then flip them over with tongs and cook for another 3 minutes, or until golden brown.
4. Remove the meatballs from the pan and set aside.

To make the sauce:

1. Add all the sauce to the same skillet you cooked the meatballs in and stir well.

2. Bring the sauce to a boil over high heat, then reduce the heat to medium and return the meatballs to the pan and stir well through the sauce.

3. Simmer the sauce for 10 minutes, or until it has thickened and reduced by about a third and the meatballs are tender.

4. Serve warm, preferably over a serving of Keto Cheddar Leek Cauliflower Mash.

11. Keto Mongolian Beef

Preparation Time: 25 min | Cooking Time: 10 min | Total Time: 35 min | Yield: 4 Servings 1x

INGREDIENTS:

- 1 ½ pounds of flank steak
- ¼ teaspoon ground red pepper flakes, optional
- 1 tablespoon of fish sauce
- 3 cloves of garlic, chopped
- 2 tablespoons gluten-free soy sauce or coconut aminos (I use this brand)
- ½ cup of golden monk fruit sweetener (I use this brand) Code PEACE for 20% off
- 1 tablespoon of avocado oil
- 1 tablespoon of grated fresh ginger

- 1 ½ teaspoons of glucomannan powder or xanthan gum
- 2 tablespoons thinly sliced green onions

DIRECTIONS:

1. Cut against the wire, cut steak into thin strips and then into 1- to 2-inch pieces. Put aside.

2. In a small bowl, combine the red pepper flakes, fish sauce, chopped garlic, soy sauce, sesame oil, and monk fruit sweetener. In a large mixing bowl, add sliced steak and turn steak strips with tongs until all meat is coated with marinade. Cover the bowl and transfer to the refrigerator to marinate for 30 minutes.

3. When the steak is done marinating, heat the avocado oil in a large saucepan over medium heat. When the oil is hot, adds the steak, marinade, and grated ginger to the pan. Cook the steak until brown, turning if necessary. Turn off the heat and remove the pan from the heat.

4. Using a spoon, scoop ½ cup of the sauce from the pan and place in a mixing bowl. Sprinkle the glucomannan powder over the sauce and whisk the together until the sauce thickens. Return the thickened sauce to the pan. Serve beef in bowls on its own or on top of cauliflower rice and garnish with sliced green onions.

12. Easy Keto Burger

Preparation Time: 15 min |Cooking Time: 30 min | Total Time: 45 min| Servings: 4 | Calories: 387kcal

INGREDIENTS:

- 1½ pounds ground beef see tips below
- 2 tablespoons of olive oil plus more for the pan
- 1 teaspoon of onion powder
- 1 teaspoon of garlic powder
- 1 teaspoon of Dijon mustard
- 1 tablespoon tomato paste sugar free - see tips below
- ½ teaspoon ground pepper
- 1 teaspoon of salt
- 3 eggs
- ½ cup of whipped cream

- 1½ cups of grated cheddar
- 3 cups canned or frozen green beans - see tips below

DIRECTIONS:

1. Grease an 8 × 8 " baking dish with olive oil and set aside. Preheat your oven to 360 ° F. Place 1½ pounds ground beef, 1 teaspoon onion powder, 1 teaspoon garlic powder, 1 teaspoon Dijon mustard, 1 tablespoon tomato paste, ½ teaspoon ground pepper and 1 teaspoon salt. Stir well until combined.

2. Ground beef and other in glass Keto burger casserole bowl

3. Heat 2 tablespoons of olive oil in a large frying pan. Add the ground beef mixture and cook for about 10 minutes, spreading while it cooks, until completely browned.

4. Brown the minced meat in a frying pan

5. Add the cooked ground beef mixture in an even layer to your prepared baking dish. Divide 3 cups of canned or frozen green beans over the meat.

6. Green beans on top of beef for Keto casserole recipe

7. In a medium bowl, beat 3 eggs. Add ½ cup of whipped cream and a pinch of salt. Pour this mixture evenly over the meat and green beans. Divide 1½ cups of shredded cheddar cheese over the beef and green bean mixture.

8. Add cheese to a Keto casserole recipe

9. Bake for 20-30 minutes, until the cheese is golden brown. Serve and   enjoy!

10. Serving a Keto casserole on a plate with a casserole dish or hamburger casserole dish

11. Comments

12. Mix with ground pork: In addition to beef, you can also use ground   pork   for   even   more flavor. Use a mixture of 1 pound ground beef and 5   ounces of ground pork if you want to use pork.

13. Sugar-Free Tomato Paste: Make sure your tomato paste is sugar-free. You can replace it with sugar-free ketchup.

14. Using frozen green beans: If you are using frozen green beans, you   don't   need   to thaw them. They will be fully cooked during the frying   pan.

15. Other Vegetables to Use: Not a fan of green beans? You can still make this easy Keto burger recipe! Instead, try using cauliflower or broccoli. Broccoli is one of our personal favorites!

13. Keto Curry Bowl With Spinach

Preparation Time: 5 min |Cooking Time: 10 min | Total Time: 15 min| Servings: 4 | Net Carbohydrates: 4g

Ingredients:

- 1/4-pound pancetta
- 1 pound ground beef
- 1 tbsp. tomato paste
- 1/2 onion
- 2 celery stalks chopped
- 2 cloves of garlic
- 1/2 c beef stock or stock
- 2 bay leaves
- salt / pepper to taste

DIRECTIONS:

1. Gently fry the sliced onion in coconut oil until the onion is cooked and clear.

2. Add the garlic and curry powder, stir and cook for another minute. Be careful not to burn the garlic.

3. Add the ground beef / mince and keep stirring until well cooked.

4. Add the coconut cream and stir.

5. While the curried beef is still simmering in the pan, start adding the chopped spinach a handful at a time. Stir the spinach into the curried beef so that it softens. Repeat until all of the spinach has been added.

6. Serve the Keto curry in bowls and enjoy! Garnish with coconut cream (optional).

14. Keto Chili Recipe

Preparation Time: 10 min |Cooking Time: 1 hour | Total Time: 1 hour 10 min| Yield: 6 Servings

INGREDIENTS:

- 1 ½ pounds ground beef
- 1 yellow onion, diced
- 1 green pepper, diced
- 1 jalapeno, finely chopped
- 1 clove of garlic, finely chopped
- ¼ cup of tomato paste
- 15 ounces of canned diced tomatoes
- 2 cups of beef stock
- 2 tablespoons chili powder
- 1 teaspoon of cumin
- 1 teaspoon of salt

DIRECTIONS:

1. Add the ground beef, onion, and bell pepper to a large deep pan and cook over medium heat, breaking the meat into pieces while cooking. Drain the fat from the pan when the meat is cooked.

2. Add the jalapeno, garlic, tomato paste, diced tomatoes, beef stock, chili powder, cumin and salt and stir.

3. Bring to a boil and simmer. Simmer for a minimum of 20 minutes, preferably an hour for the best flavor and texture.

4. Serve with sour cream and grated cheddar, as desired

15. Ground beef stroganoff

Cooking Time: 20 min | Total Time: 30 min|

Servings: 6 | Calories: 360kcal

INGREDIENTS:

- 3 cups of chopped yellow onions
- 2 tablespoons of chopped garlic
- 1 tablespoon of ground turmeric
- 2 teaspoons grated fresh ginger
- 1 ½ teaspoons ground coriander
- 1 teaspoon of cumin powder
- 3 tablespoons of tomato paste
- 3 cups of unsalted beef stock

DIRECTIONS:

1. Add a little oil and the mushrooms in a piping hot pot and let the mushrooms fry well.

2. Then add the onion, minced meat and garlic. Season with generous salt and pepper. Let the minced meat brown and the onions soft. Stir occasionally to prevent burning. About 10 minutes.

3. Then add the Dijon mustard and the beef stock and bring to the boil.

4. Remove from heat and stir in sour cream. Add salt if necessary.

5. Garnish with fresh parsley.

16. Lamb & Beef Balti

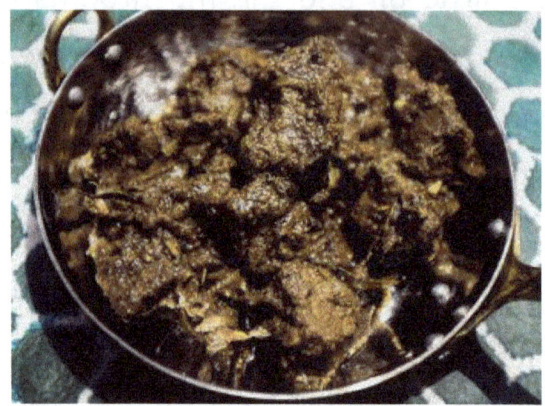

Active Time: 25 mins | Total Time: 40 mins|

Servings: 4

INGREDIENTS:

- 1 ½ cups of water
- 1 cup of brown basmati rice
- 8 grams of lean ground beef
- 8 grams of ground lamb
- 3 cups of chopped yellow onions
- 2 tablespoons of chopped garlic
- 1 tablespoon of ground turmeric
- 2 teaspoons grated fresh ginger
- 1 ½ teaspoons ground coriander
- 1 teaspoon of cumin powder
- 3 tablespoons of tomato paste
- 3 cups of unsalted beef stock

- 2 tablespoons Worcestershire sauce
- ¾ teaspoon of salt
- ¼ cup of low-fat Greek yogurt
- 3 tablespoons of chopped fresh cilantro

DIRECTIONS:

1. Combine water and rice in a medium saucepan; bring to a boil over high heat. Reduce heat and simmer, cover and cook until water is absorbed, about 40 minutes.

2. Meanwhile, cook beef and Lamb in a large skillet over medium heat, crumbling with a wooden spoon, until no longer pink, 5 to 6 minutes. Add onions and cook, stirring occasionally, until translucent, 6 to 8 minutes.

3. Increase the heat to high. Add garlic, turmeric, ginger, coriander and cumin; cook, stir fry, until fragrant, about 1 minute. Stir in the tomato paste and cook for 1 minute, stirring. Stir in stock, Worcestershire, and salt; bring to a boil. Reduce heat to medium and simmer, stirring occasionally, for 13 to 15 minutes until thick.

4. Serve the Balti over the rice, topped with some yogurt and coriander with naan bread on the side.

17. Keto Stuffed Pepper Recipe

Preparation Time: 15 mins |Cooking Time: 30 mins | Total Time: 45 mins| Servings: 6 | Calories: 388kcal

INGREDIENTS:

- 1 tablespoon of olive oil
- 1 small onion cut into cubes
- Crushed 2 cloves of garlic
- 1 pound ground beef
- 2 tablespoons of Cajun seasoning
- 1 teaspoon of salt
- 1/2 teaspoon ground pepper
- 1/2 cup of tomato passata
- 1 cup of cauliflower rice
- 6 medium peppers
- 1 cup of cheddar cheese shredded

- Common in the US - metric

DIRECTIONS:

1. Preheat your oven to 200C / 390F. Place a large saucepan over high heat and add the oil, onion and garlic. Sauté until the onion starts to turn translucent.
2. Add the ground beef and fry until brown, and then add the Cajun seasoning, salt, pepper, and tomato passata. Mix well.
3. Reduce the heat and let the mixture simmer for 5 minutes.
4. Remove from heat, stir in cauliflower rice and set aside.
5. Prepare the peppers by cutting off the top and removing the seeds and white pith from the inside. Place them in a baking dish with the cut sides facing up.
6. Spoon the ground beef mixture evenly between the peppers and top with cheddar cheese.
7. Bake in the oven for 15-20 minutes until the cheese is brown and the peppers are soft.
8. Serve immediately.

18. Beef liver with bacon recipe

Preparation Time: 10 mins |Cooking Time: 30 mins | Total Time: 40 mins| Servings: 4 | Calories: 297kcal

INGREDIENTS:

- 1-pound grass-fed beef liver
- 4 strips of bacon we use Garrett Valley Uncured Bacon
- Use 3 tablespoons of meadow butter, divided
- ½ large onion
- 4 large cloves of garlic
- 10 grams of sliced mushrooms

DIRECTIONS:

1. Remove the beef liver from the packaging and lay it flat on a paper towel. Pat dry.

2. Generously salt and pepper the liver and let it sit at room temperature while you prepare the remaining *Ingredients.*

3. Dice the bacon and fry in 2 tablespoons butter in a large skillet. When they are crispy, remove the bacon from the pan and drain on kitchen paper. Leave the fat and butter in the pan.

4. Chop the onion coarsely. You want your onion pieces to be about the same size as a piece of liver. The one-to-one ratio is part of the taste secret! Fry on low in bacon fat and butter until it starts to soften but is not yet translucent.

5. Simple beef liver recipe

6. Add garlic to the onions for another 30 seconds.

7. Add mushrooms to the onions and garlic. Fry everything until the mushrooms are cooked.

8. Simple delivery receiver

9. Move all vegetables to one side of the pan, away from the heat. You may want to screw the pan on so that that side is slightly away from the burner.

10. Reduce heat to medium and add the last tablespoon of butter.

11. When the butter has melted, add half of the liver slices. Cook until you start to see the edges cook. They change from red to gray. When that rim is a few millimeters thick (2-3 minutes, or so), flip them over.

12. Fry for another 2-3 minutes on the other side. Until you know how you like your liver, the best way to check it is by cutting it. If it is still red, keep turning until it is barely cooked. You just want a hint of pink so it's cooked through yet soft.

13. Place the liver on a platter and cook the remaining liver in the same way.

14. Toss the bacon cubes through the vegetables and spread the liver with it.

19. Keto Burrito Peppers

Active Time: 15 min | Total Time: 1 hour |
Yield: Serve: 4 (portion size: 1 stuffed bell
pepper)

INGREDIENTS:

- 1 pound ground beef
- ½ cup diced red onion
- 1 teaspoon chili powder
- ¾ teaspoon of kosher salt
- ½ teaspoon of cumin powder
- 2 cups of cauliflower rice
- 1 (5-oz.) Can diced green chilies
- 4 ounces Cheddar cheese, grated (about 1 cup), divided
- 4 tablespoons chopped fresh cilantro, divided

- 4 large bell peppers (any color) or poblano chilies, tops, seeds, and membranes removed
- 4 tablespoons of prepared salsa with no added sugar, divided
- 1 avocado, sliced
- Lime wedges

DIRECTIONS:

1. Preheat the oven to 350 ° F. Heat a large skillet over medium heat. Add ground beef; cook, stirring often to crumble, until browned, about 6 minutes. Add onion and cook, stirring often, until onion softens, about 3 minutes. Add chili powder, salt and cumin; cook, stirring often, until fragrant, about 1 minute.

2. Add cauliflower and cook until tender, about 4 minutes. Stir in green chilies and remove from heat. Stir in 3/4 cup of cheese and 3 tablespoons of cilantro.

3. Generously fill each bell pepper with beef mixture and cover each with 1 tablespoon of salsa. Place the peppers in a 20-inch baking dish and cover with aluminum foil. Bake for 40 minutes in the preheated oven. Remove foil and cover evenly with the remaining cheese. Bake for about 10 minutes until golden and fizzy. Finish with slices of avocado. Sprinkle with the remaining cilantro and serve with lime wedges.

20. Keto Meat Pie

Preparation Time: 30 mins |Cooking Time: 40 mins | Servings: 6

INGREDIENTS:

Meat stuffing

- ½ yellow onion, finely chopped
- 1 clove of garlic, finely chopped
- 2 tbsp. butter or olive oil
- 1¼ pound ground beef or ground turkey
- 2 tbsp. dried oregano or dried basil
- ½ teaspoon of salt
- ¼ tsp. ground black pepper
- 3 tbsp. tomato paste
- ½ cup of water

Pie crust

- ¾ cup (3 oz.) Almond flour
- ¼ cup (1¼ oz.) Sesame seeds
- ¼ cup (¾ oz.) Coconut flour
- 1 tablespoon of ground psyllium husk powder
- 1 tsp. baking powder
- 1 pinch of salt
- 3 tbsp. olive oil
- 1 large egg
- ¼ cup of water

Topping

- 1 cup of cottage cheese
- 1 cup (4 oz.) Cheddar cheese, shredded

DIRECTIONS:

1. Meat stuffing
2. Preheat the oven to 350 ° F (175 ° C).
3. Heat the butter or olive oil in a large skillet over medium heat. Add the onion and cook for a few minutes. Add the garlic, minced meat, oregano or basil, salt and pepper. Use a spatula to break the meat into smaller pieces while stirring. Cook for 8-10 minutes or until no longer pink.

4. Add the tomato paste, water and stir to combine. Reduce heat to medium-low and simmer uncovered for 20 minutes, stirring occasionally. Meanwhile make the pie crust.

5. Pie crust

6. Mix the crust with a food processor or fork.

7. Place a round piece of baking paper in a well-greased 23-25 cm spring form pan or a deep cake pan. Use a spatula or well-greased fingers to press the dough evenly onto the bottom and sides of the pan Pierce the bottom and sides of the crust with a fork to prevent bubbling.

8. Pre-bake the crust for 10 minutes. Remove from oven and place the meat mixture in the crust.

9. In a small bowl, mix the cottage cheese and grated cheese. Spread on the cake.

10. Bake on the lower rack for 30-40 minutes, or until golden brown in color.

11. Low in ketogenic carbohydrates

21. Easy Pork Crawler Recipe With Vegetables (Low Carb)

Cooking Time: 5 mins | Total Time: 15 mins|

Servings: 4 | Calories: 266kcal

INGREDIENTS:

- 3/4-pound pork loin, cut into thin strips
- 2 tablespoons avocado or olive oil (divided)
- 1 tablespoon of fresh ground ginger
- 1 teaspoon of chopped garlic
- 12 ounces of broccoli florets
- 1 red pepper, cut into strips
- 1 bunch green onions (scallions), in pieces of 2-inch cut

- 2 tablespoons Tamari soy sauce (or coconut aminos)
- 1 tablespoon of extra dry sherry
- 1 1/2 tablespoons low-carb sugar (or sugar or coconut sugar)
- 1 teaspoon cornstarch (or arrowroot)
- 1 teaspoon of sesame oil

DIRECTIONS:

1. Preparation: Finely chop a clove of garlic. Cut a 2.5 cm piece of ginger and peel the thin skin with a spoon. Finely chop the ginger and add it to the garlic. Cut the pork tenderloin into thin strips and mix with 1 tbsp. oil and the ginger and garlic.

2. Cut the red pepper into strips and place in the bottom of a medium bowl. Cut the green onions (scallions) into 2-inch pieces, including some of the green stems, and add them to the bowl. Cut the broccoli florets into large, bite-sized pieces and place on top.

3. Add the sweetener and cornstarch (arrowroot) to a small bowl and mix. Stir in Tamari soy sauce, dry sherry and sesame oil.

4. Method: Put the wok on high heat. It is ready when a drop of water jumps over the surface. Add 1 tablespoon of oil and quickly tilt the wok to cover all surfaces. Pour out the remaining oil. Return the wok to the heat and add the pork to the sides and bottom of the pan. Leave the pork alone until it is cooked through halfway through the cooking time; the bottom half turns white. Stir the pork and cook until almost done. Remove from pan to serving bowl.

5. Dump the bowl of vegetables into the wok with the broccoli on the bottom. Cover with a lid and cook for 1 minute. Stir the vegetables and return the pork and any juices to the pan. Stir the pork and vegetables together. Stir in the stir-fry sauce and pour it over the pork and vegetables. Move the pork stir-fry aside and let the sauce cook in the bottom of the wok, stirring occasionally for a few seconds until the sauce thickens.

6. If you want the sauce to be thicker, remove the stir-fried pork and vegetables from the serving bowl and let the sauce cook a little longer. When the sauce has reached the desired consistency, pour the sauce over the stir-fry. Serve.

22. Keto Stuffed Pork Tenderloin with Mushroom Sauce

Preparation Time: 10 mins |Cooking Time: 40 mins | Total Time: 40mins| Yield: 4

INGREDIENTS:

- 1 pound of pork tenderloin
- 2 tablespoons of oil
- 3 slices of provolone cheese
- 1/3 cup of freshly chopped spinach
- salt and pepper to taste
- 1 teaspoon of crushed garlic
- 8 oz. mushrooms sliced
- 1 tablespoon of balsamic vinegar
- 1 large clove of garlic, finely chopped
- 2 tablespoons of butter

- 1 teaspoon better than stock beef mixed with 1 cup of water (or 1 cup of beef stock)
- 1 tablespoon of whipped cream

DIRECTIONS:

1. Preheat the oven to 375 degrees F.
2. Cut the pork tenderloin lengthwise but leave 1/2 inch so you can open it like a book.
3. Wrap the meat in plastic and pound thinly to about 1/4 - 1/2 inches thick.
4. Sprinkle chopped garlic and salt and pepper over the meat.
5. Layer the cheese slices and then the spinach.
6. Roll up tightly lengthwise and secure with string or toothpicks.
7. Heat oil in a pan and fry the meat for about 5 minutes on each side.
8. Put in the oven and cook for about 25 minutes.
9. In the meantime, add butter and mushrooms to a large sauté pan and cook for about 5 minutes.
10. Add the garlic and stock and cook for another 5 minutes until slightly reduced.
11. Add the vinegar and mix well. Then add the cream and mix.

12. When the meat comes out of the oven, let it stand for 10 minutes and then pour mushroom sauce over it

23. Keto Short Ribs recipe

Preparation Time: 10 mins |Cooking Time: 1 hour |Yield: 3 Servings | Calories: 860kcal | Net Carbs: 6g|

INGREDIENTS:

- 1 pound ribs meat
- 1 tbsp. butter
- 1/2 onion
- salt / pepper to taste

DIRECTIONS:

1. Prepare Short Ribs: Pat short ribs dry with kitchen paper. Season all sides generously with salt and pepper.

2. Brown Short Ribs: Select the sauté mode on the pressure cooker (Note 3) for medium heat. Add olive oil to coat the bottom of the pot. Add butter and stir until melted.

3. Once the pot has reached temperature (display shows HOT), add short ribs in a single layer. Without moving them, cook them for about 7 minutes until the bottom is nicely browned. Turnover and cook the other side for about 5 minutes. Place the browned short ribs on the plate.

4. Cook Aromatics: Add carrots, shallots and garlic to the pot. Cook for a few minutes until the shallots start to brown, stirring frequently. Turn off sauté mode. Add red wine and stir, use a wooden spoon to loosen flavorful brown bits stuck to the bottom of the pan.

5. Add short ribs to the pot in a single layer. Top with fresh thyme sprigs. Season with extra salt and pepper.

6. Pressure cooker: close the lid. Boil under high pressure for 45 minutes, followed by natural release for 15 minutes. Manually release the remaining pressure.

7. Discover and transfer ribs only to serving plates. Skim off and discard any fat in the remaining liquid; this reduces the amount of oil in the final sauce.

8. Thicken Sauce: Turn on sauté mode and add balsamic vinegar. Boil the liquid to a slightly sticky sauce, 10 to 15 minutes, stirring occasionally. Turn off sauté mode. Spoon the sauce on the short ribs and serve.

24. Easy Cheesy Low Carb Keto Spinach Artichoke Dip Recipe

Preparation Time: 10 mins |Cooking Time: 30 mins |Total Time: 40 mins

INGREDIENTS:

- 4 oz. Spinach (chopped)
- 4 oz. cream cheese
- 2 tablespoons of mayonnaise
- 2 tablespoons sour cream (or an additional 2 tablespoons mayonnaise)
- 1/4 cup of grated Parmesan cheese
- 1 can (14.5 oz.) artichoke hearts in water (drained, chopped, and pressed to release extra moisture)
- 4 cloves of garlic (finely chopped)
- 1/4 teaspoon black pepper

- 2/3 cup mozzarella cheese (shredded, divided into 2 parts)

DIRECTIONS:

1. Heat a greased pan over medium heat. Add the chopped spinach. Cook, stirring occasionally, until the spinach is limp and bright green. (You can also simmer the spinach in the microwave for 2-3 minutes.) Set aside to cool. If you want to speed up the cooling, you can place the bowl in a larger bowl of ice (optional).

2. While the spinach is cooling, preheat the oven to 350 degrees F (177 degrees C).

3. Meanwhile, heat the cream cheese in the microwave or in a small saucepan on the stove over low heat. Once it has melted enough to stir, add the mayonnaise, sour cream, grated Parmesan, chopped artichoke hearts, chopped garlic, black pepper, and half of the grated mozzarella. Stir to combine.

4. When the spinach is cool enough to handle, gather it into a ball and squeeze it a few times, making sure to get as much water out as possible. Add the spinach to the artichoke mixture.

5. Transfer the dip to a small ceramic appetizer dish or large bowl. Smooth the top with a spatula. Sprinkle with the remaining grated mozzarella.

6. Bake for about 30 minutes, until warm and bubbly. Serve warm.

25. Keto Stuffed Meatballs Cheese

Preparation Time: 10 mins |Cooking Time: 24 mins |Yield: 18 meats | Total Time: 34 mins|

INGREDIENTS:

- 1 pound ground beef (I get grass-fed ground beef from Butcher Box)
- 1 pound of Italian sausage
- 1 teaspoon of black pepper
- 1 teaspoon of dried oregano
- 1 teaspoon of garlic powder
- 3 mozzarella cheese sticks, cut into 1-inch pieces
- 2 tablespoons of avocado oil
- 1 jar low-carb marinara sauce (Mezzetta has an option for 6 cars per serving)

- 1 cup of low-fat, low-moisture mozzarella cheese
- 1 tablespoon parsley, chopped (for garnish)

DIRECTIONS:

1. In a large mixing bowl, combine ground beef, Italian sausage, salt, black pepper, dried oregano, and garlic powder.
2. Pour avocado oil into an oven-safe pan, making sure the entire bottom of the pan is covered with oil.
3. Grab about 1/4 cups (give or take some) of the meat mixture and put in a piece of the mozzarella cheese, then roll it into a ball. Place the meatball in the prepared ovenproof pan. Repeat until the meat is finished.
4. Set the oven to Grill and place the pan in the oven for about 12 minutes, or until the meatballs turn a nice golden brown on top.
5. Remove the pan from the oven and pour the marinara sauce over the meatballs. Then sprinkle the mozzarella cheese on top.

6. Return the pan to the oven and turn the oven to Bake at 350 degrees and bake for an additional 12 minutes, or until the internal temperature of the meatballs reaches 160 degrees.
7. Carefully remove the pan from the oven and garnish with chopped parsley.

26. Keto Asparagus Fries

Preparation Time: 20 mins |Cooking Time: 10 mins |Rest Time: 30 mins | Total Time: 1 hour

INGREDIENTS:

- 1 pound asparagus trimmed (thick if possible)
- Salt and pepper to taste
- 1 cup of Parmesan cheese
- 3/4 cup of almond flour
- 1/4 teaspoon of cayenne pepper
- 1/4 teaspoon baking powder
- 4 beaten eggs
- Oil spray I used avocado oil

DIRECTIONS:

1. Prick the asparagus with a fork. Season with at least 1/2 teaspoon of salt. Place them on kitchen paper and let them stand for 30 minutes.

2. Meanwhile, combine 1 cup of Parmesan cheese, almond flour, cayenne, and baking powder in a bowl. Season with salt and pepper. (I use 1/4 tsp. each.)

3. Beat the egg in a separate bowl.

4. Dip the asparagus in the eggs and cover with the cheese mixture.

5. Preheat your air fryer to 400 degrees.

6. Arrange the asparagus in a single layer and cook in batches if necessary. Spray well with oil. Let it boil for 5 minutes. Turnover and spray again. Cook another 4 to 5 minutes, until the asparagus is tender.

7. Fried Asparagus Fries

8. Preheat and oven to 420 degrees. Cover a baking tray with parchment paper.

9. Arrange the asparagus in a single layer. Spray with oil. Bake for 15 to 20 minutes.

27. Keto Stuffed Mushrooms With Sausage

Preparation Time: 15 min |Cooking Time: 25 min |Yield: about 20 |Total Time: 40 min|

INGREDIENTS:

- 1 pound of mild Italian sausage
- 1 pound of cremini mushrooms
- 4 oz. cream cheese
- 1/3 cup of grated mozzarella
- salt, if necessary
- 1/2 tsp. red pepper flakes
- 1/4 cup of grated Parmesan cheese

DIRECTIONS:

1. Preheat the oven to 350F. Clean the mushrooms and remove the stems.
2. Fry the sausage in a large skillet over medium heat. Once cooked, remove it in a large mixing bowl.
3. Add the cream cheese and mozzarella cheese and stir to mix. Taste to season and add salt and red pepper if necessary.
4. Spoon the sausage mixture into the mushroom caps. Sprinkle with Parmesan cheese. Place them in an oven-proof frying pan or baking dish.
5. Bake for 25 minutes, until the mushrooms are soft and the cheese is brown.

28.Shrimp Rangoon Mini Paprika

Preparation Time: 30 mins |Cooking Time: 10 mins |Total Time: 40 mins|

INGREDIENTS:

- 15 mini peppers cut in half, seeds and pith removed
- ½ lb. raw shrimp peeled, tail removed, gutted
- 1 teaspoon chili powder
- ¼ teaspoon of garlic powder
- ¼ teaspoon of salt or more to taste
- 1 tablespoon of olive oil
- 120ml room temperature cream cheese (full fat is best, but light cream cheese will work too)
- 2 tablespoons of chopped green onions

- 1 teaspoon of lime juice
- ⅓ cup of finely chopped Gouda or white Cheddar cheese (about 3 ounces)
- olive oil spray or extra olive oil for brushing the baking tray

DIRECTIONS:

1. Preheat the oven to 350F. Spray a large baking sheet with nonstick cooking spray or brush with olive oil.
2. In a medium bowl, combine the shrimp, chili powder, garlic powder, and salt. Mix well. Heat the olive oil in a large frying pan and cook the shrimp over high heat for 2 minutes per side, or until tender. Set aside to cool.
3. Coarsely chop the cooked shrimp into small pieces.
4. In a medium bowl, combine the chopped shrimp, room temperature cream cheese, chopped green onions, and lime juice. Mix well. Taste it and add salt and pepper if necessary.

5. Fill each bell pepper half with about ½ - 1 tablespoon of the cream cheese mixture and press down gently to fill the bell pepper. Place the mini peppers on the baking tray. Sprinkle a pinch of grated cheese on each mini pepper. Bake at 350F for 10 minutes. Remove from heat and let cool 10 minutes before serving.

29. Smoked trout mousse

Preparation Time: 10 mins | Total Time: 10 mins | Portion: 2

INGREDIENTS:

- 2 ounces smoked trout, peeled and boned (or smoked mackerel)
- 1.5 grams of unsalted butter softened
- 0.38 teaspoon of horseradish prepared, not creamy
- 0.75 tablespoons of whipped cream
- 0.75 tablespoons of lemon juice
- Kosher salt and white pepper to taste
- Fresh chives finely chopped, (optional)
- Fresh dill finely chopped (optional)

DIRECTIONS

1. In the bowl of a food processor, pulse trout for 10-15 seconds

2. Add butter and pulse for another 5-10 seconds.

3. Add cream, horseradish, lemon juice, and herbs and pulse until mousse is blended, but not completely smooth, about 10 to 20 seconds.

4. Taste and adjust seasoning with additional lemon juice, salt, and white pepper as needed.

5. Garnish with fresh chives or dill.

30.Crack Dip Recipe With Bacon And Cream Cheese

Preparation Time: 10 mins |Cooking Time: 15 mins |Total Time: 25 mins

INGREDIENTS:

- 8 oz. cream cheese
- 3/4 cup Ranch Dressing (for a thick dressing; use 2/3 cup if using a thin dressing)
- 1/3 cup of sour cream
- 1 cup Cheddar cheese (shredded)
- 1/3 cup Bacon pieces (cooked)
- 1/3 cup green onions (chopped)
- 1/8 teaspoon cayenne pepper (optional - or more to taste)

DIRECTIONS:

1. Preheat the oven to 350 degrees F (177 degrees C).

2. Gently heat the cream cheese in the microwave on medium power, or on the stove in a double boiler, until warm and easy to stir. (Don't let it get piping hot, just keep it warm. If it's too hot, wait for it to cool just to be just warm for the next step, to keep the ranch and sour cream from curling.)

3. Stir the ranch dressing into the cream cheese until smooth, then stir in the sour cream. Stir in the remaining

4. Transfer the dip to a 1/2-liter (1/2 liter) glass or stoneware baking dish, such as this one.

5. Bake for about 15 minutes, until hot and bubbly on the edges below. Serve warm or warm, with vegetables or low-carb crackers.

31. Baked Salami Mozzarella Bites

Preparation Time: 15 min |Cooking Time: 20 min |Total Time: 35 min | Servings: 32 bites

INGREDIENTS:

- 8 sticks of mozzarella cheese, cut in half lengthwise and then cut in half crosswise
- 32 square wonton wraps
- 32 slices of salami
- olive oil
- To serve
- chopped fresh parsley, for garnish
- pizza, marinara or spaghetti sauce for dipping

DIRECTIONS:

1. Preheat the oven to 400 degrees F. Line a baking tray with parchment paper.

2. Place a piece of salami in the bottom corner of the wonton wrapper and put a piece of cheese on top. Wrap tightly like a burrito, by folding the bottom corner over the cheese, rolling a turn, folding the sides in, and rolling it further (make sure the cheese is tight to prevent leaking). Dampen the remaining corner with water to seal.

3. Repeat the process with all wonton wraps; put them on the baking tray and brush them lightly with olive oil.

4. Bake for 12-15 minutes until golden brown; turn and bake for another 5 minutes. Let it cool for a few minutes.

5. Serve with dipping sauce of your choice and enjoy!

32.Keto Shrimp Guacamole and Bacon

Preparation Time: 20 min |Cooking Time: 20 min |Total Time: 40 min | Servings: 20 | Calories: 60kcal

INGREDIENTS:

For the Guacamole:

- 2 small avocados
- 1/2 cup chopped red onion
- 1/2 lime, squeezed
- 1/3 cup of fresh cilantro lightly packed
- 1/2 teaspoon of salt

For the shrimp:

- 10 ounces of large raw shrimp, peeled and gutted, yield 20 shrimp
- 1/2 teaspoon of salt
- 1/4 teaspoon of pepper
- 1/2 teaspoon of cumin
- 2 tablespoons of butter

DIRECTIONS:

1. Make the Guacamole
2. Add all for the guacamole to a food processor and pulse until combined.
3. You want the guacamole to be a little thick. Taste for spices and adjust to your taste.
4. Boil the shrimp
5. Season both sides of the shrimp with salt, pepper and cumin.
6. Heat the butter in a large skillet over medium heat.
7. Sear the shrimp on both sides until they are no longer opaque.
8. Remove the pan from the heat and set aside.
9. Place the cucumber slices on a plate and season with salt.

10. Top with a slice of bacon, followed by a spoonful of guacamole.
11. Finish with a shrimp and secure with a toothpick.

33.Keto Chips with Sour Cream and Onion

Yield | Preparation Time: 15 min |Cooking Time: 10 min |Total Time: 25 min | Servings: 32 bites

INGREDIENTS:

- 1 ¾ cups of grated mozzarella cheese
- 2 tbsp. salted butter
- 1 large egg
- 2 tbsp. sour cream
- ¾ cups of finely ground blanched almond flour
- ½ tsp. onion powder
- ½ tsp. garlic powder
- ½ tsp. mustard powder
- ½ tsp. sea salt (more to taste)
- 1 tbsp. chopped chives

DIRECTIONS:

1. Preheat the oven to 350 degrees Fahrenheit and prepare two baking trays with silicone liners or parchment paper.

2. Place the grated mozzarella and butter in a microwave-safe bowl and microwave for 1-2 minutes until the cheese is completely melted.

3. Mix well with a handheld or standing mixer. Then add the egg and the sour cream and mix well.

4. Add the almond flour, garlic powder, onion powder, mustard powder and salt. Mix it until everything is evenly distributed and a dough form.

5. Mix in the chives and put the dough in the fridge to cool while you prepare the parchment paper.

6. Spray two large baking tray-sized pieces of parchment paper with coconut or avocado oil. Or brush it up with a basting brush. Place the dough between the two pieces of paper (oil in the middle so that the dough does not stick).

7. Take out a rolling pin and roll out the dough as thinly as possible between the two pieces of parchment paper.

8. Remove the paper from the top and cut into triangles or desired shapes. Carefully peel off the dough triangles and place on a baking tray lined with baking paper or silicone liners.

9. Bake in the 350-degree oven for 8-10 minutes or until edges start to brown. The browner they are, the crisper they will be, but be careful not to burn them.

10. Let cool and serve with your favorite dip or soup or enjoy it yourself.

Conclusion

Finish here this food guide and the collection of recipes prepared for you. Also, I would like to thank you for going through these recipes. Hope these will help you maintaining a healthy life schedule.

I wish you good luck!

CPSIA information can be obtained
at www.ICGtesting.com
Printed in the USA
LVHW081151150521
687531LV00009B/442